Practicing Oral History with Immigrant Narrators

Practicing Oral History Series

Series Editor

Nancy MacKay, San Jose State University

Museums, historical societies, libraries, classrooms, cultural institutions, alumni associations, and neighborhood groups are among the growing list of organizations that use oral history to document their own communities. At present, there are no handy resources for these professionals to plan and implement an oral history project within their own professional frameworks.

The Left Coast series Practicing Oral History fills this gap. Series titles consist of concise, instructive books that address the special circumstances of oral history within a specific user community. Each title provides practical tools for conducting and presenting an oral history project that conforms to the best practices of the Oral History Association but targets the particular needs of a community.

Practicing Oral History in Historical Organizations, Barbara W. Sommer

Practicing Oral History with Immigrant Narrators, Carol McKirdy

Curating Oral Histories, Second Edition: From Interview to Archive, Nancy MacKay

Story Bridges: A Guide for Conducting Intergenerational Oral History Projects, Angela Zusman

For more information on these publications, or to order, go to www.LCoastPress.com

PRACTICING ORAL HISTORY WITH IMMIGRANT NARRATORS

Carol McKirdy

Walnut Creek, California

LEFT COAST PRESS, INC.
1630 North Main Street, #400
Walnut Creek, CA 94596
www.LCoastPress.com

ISBN 978-1-62958-003-6 hardback
ISBN 978-1-62958-004-3 paperback
ISBN 978-1-62958-005-0 institutional eBook
ISBN 978-1-62958-006-7 consumer eBook

Library of Congress Cataloging-in-Publication Data on file.

Printed in the United States of America

♾™ The paper used in this publication meets the minimum requirements of American National Standard for Information Sciences—Permanence of Paper for Printed Library Materials, ANSI/NISO Z39.48–1992.

CONTENTS

FOREWORD

There has never been a better time for oral history. The methodology developed in the latter half of the twentieth century by and for academics has laid the foundation for a new generation of practitioners whose innovative ideas and comfort with technology put a twenty-first-century spin on the field. Museum curators, public historians, teachers, artists, scientists, and activists are some of the user communities who apply oral history to their work. Most of these practitioners don't have the time or interest for an in-depth study of methodology; they want the tools to create the best oral histories possible within the framework of their own professions.

The *Practicing Oral History* series is designed for these readers. Each volume is organized to give the reader a snapshot of some aspect of applied oral history, providing the context for the topic, the tools and best practices for applying oral history to their own work, and how to find additional expertise when needed. Each book is self-contained, giving the reader the necessary methodology, context, and practical tools between the covers, without an overload of information.

No matter where in the world we live, we feel the impact of globalization. Many of us were born in a different country from the one we reside in. And if not, it is likely that our parents, our children, our neighbors, our teachers, or our doctors were. This enormous population migration in recent history throws into high relief the fact that for each of us, no matter where we live, the face of our nation and our community is very different from the one that our grandparents knew.

Author Carol McKirdy provides statistics to substantiate that. For example, in her home state of New South Wales, Australia, *residents* come from 225 different birthplaces and have 245 different ancestries, speak over 215 languages, and practice 125 different religions. The Australian census statistics indicate that forty-seven percent of the population was either born overseas or has a parent that was born overseas, while the United States reports thirteen percent (41.3 million immigrants) and the United Kingdom reports twelve percent (7.5 million immigrants).

Every immigrant has a story we can learn from, and the very best way for their stories to reach the ears and the hearts of public audiences is through the recorded oral history interview. *Practicing Oral History with Immigrant Narrators* provides the tools and best practices to do just that. McKirdy honors the uniqueness of every immigrant's story, sensitively illustrated with real-life examples, and at the same time recognises commonalities within the immigrant experience. Her chapters on insider/outsider interaction, culture, language, and trauma will be valuable to anyone working with immigrants. Other chapters, especially "How to Do an Oral History Project Step by Step," will guide readers through the nuts and bolts of doing oral history. The book as a whole serves as a one-stop shop for any practitioners working with immigrant oral history.

Author Carol McKirdy draws on her oral history work among immigrant populations in Australia as well as her twenty-five years as an adult educator teaching immigrants English language and literacy skills. She notes that her home state of New South Wales, Australia, is the most culturally and linguistically diverse community in the world, providing her with a panorama of multicultural life in her daily life. The example and case studies from immigrant oral history projects in Australia and the United States enliven the text and make for wonderful reading; in fact, this is one of the few oral history methodology books that may bring the reader to tears. *Practicing Oral History with Immigrant Narrators* is a wonderful contribution to the practice of oral history and, indirectly, will make a giant step toward giving voice to the immigrants that form such an important part of the history of our time.

Nancy MacKay
Berkeley, California
February 2015

PREFACE

"Retell Record Retain"

Practicing Oral History with Immigrant Narrators considers the specific preparation and planning required when recording the narratives of people with an *immigrant* background, especially people who are not proficient English speakers. The book builds on standard techniques, methods, and processes oral historians have established to record *oral history*, but is customised and sensitive to the needs of a particular demographic—the immigrant *narrator*. The book aims to be a practical guide that adds to our knowledge about oral history *projects* that have a specialised focus, such as those for family, *community*, church, school, institution, and business histories, among others.

Historical *record* making is not limited to leaders and decision makers, victors, heroes, celebrities, and champions. Oral history validates and records ordinary life. An ordinary person's history and remembrances of the past can be recorded comparatively easily through the procedures used in an oral history project and *interview*. Oral history narratives are interesting, illuminating, informative, often funny, and often sad. Oral history shows how people have experienced the past or events of the past or how they remember their experiences. It also highlights individual interpretations and perspectives of the past. Any person's recollection of the past might be important to record, and almost everyone has a story to tell. Immigrant narratives are everyday stories about everyday people; they may be boat people, *refugees, asylum seekers*, and people who, for whatever reason, made the journey to a new country and life. Their stories of the everyday are of extraordinary voices telling extraordinary tales. Many of their stories are powerful in their ability to make us wonder at the determination of people who persevere against adversity and difference to make new lives. Seeking out immigrant histories is important because having a different native language can isolate people from having their narratives heard.

My practical experience as an oral historian has been in Australia. Australia is a multicultural nation; forty-seven percent[1] of people were either born overseas or have a parent born overseas, and often English is not the native language. I have specific experience in recording the oral histories of narrators for whom English is not the native tongue. As well, I am a dually qualified professional; for more than twenty-five years I've worked as an adult educator teaching adults, mostly immigrants, who lack basic English language and literacy skills. I have first-hand experience of the difficulties *migrants* encounter because of a lack of English language proficiency and the difficulties of adjusting to life in a different country. From two professional stances I have gathered knowledge based on working, communicating, and liaising with, as well as learning from, people who have come from another country. I have developed and learned effective techniques, approaches, and considerations for recording the oral history of an immigrant narrator.

Of course, not all immigrant narrators find speaking English in an oral history interview difficult. Immigrant narrators may have emigrated from an English-speaking country or they may have acquired native or near-native proficiency in English. A narrator's spoken English may be excellent, so potential difficulties caused by a lack of language expertise are just as irrelevant as for a narrator for whom English is the first language. Many narrators are bilingual or multilingual. However, regardless of the difficulties of language barriers, immigrants might require special consideration in an oral history interview because of their immigrant background. This book considers the special issues related to this particular group of narrators.

Immigrant narrators are like most people in relation to oral history; they have their memories recorded for many reasons. They want family history conserved; they don't want customs forgotten; they want their children to know what they experienced; they want special circumstances and occasions recorded, historical events documented, and accents and unique ways of speaking preserved; or they want the stories behind personally relevant photographs, images, objects, and items recorded, amongst other motives. Immigrant narrators might also know significant history that should be recorded. They may know a great deal about public events in their former countries that should be documented because there is no other way of learning about it. Frequently they have emigrated from countries experiencing war, civil unrest, human rights violations, poverty, and diaspora. Immigrants have frequently been witnesses to events of historical importance and significance. They have often participated in these events, and their first-hand memories may add a very different perspective to mainstream historical accounts. Many immigrants have worked hard in their new home and have made respected and appreciated contributions to all facets of society—economic, civic, and social—and permanent records of these stories are valuable and important. An immigrant oral history project may also involve recording the lives of elders in the community, who emigrated a generation or more ago, before irreplaceable and irretrievable stories are lost.

Due to a limited capacity to engage in community activities, someone for whom understanding and speaking English is difficult or not fully developed, and living in a new country, either newly arrived or as a long-term resident, could easily be overlooked by oral history project designers. Important immigrant histories that should be retold and recorded for future generations may either not be collected or the oral history process may not be as effective as possible because of an *interviewer's* lack of understanding of best practice procedures for people with an immigrant background.

This book intends to give both the novice and experienced oral historian insights into the needs of an immigrant narrator and the skills and confidence to effectively scope and execute an oral history project of any size with narrators who have come from another country or for people tracing their heritage to another culture. It has practical advice informed by the existing theoretical work in oral history and aims to assist project designers and interviewers to gain the skills required. This book covers important considerations to ensure an "immigrant" oral history project is successful. For example, people who have emigrated may have experienced trauma, and this warrants very special attention for everyone involved. There are practical strategies to follow for people for whom communicating in English is feasible but challenging, and procedures for using interpreters. The idiosyncrasies of English for non-native speakers are explored in relation to doing an oral history project. The book also looks at cultural influences and how to work with immigrant communities. There are descriptions of five Australian and American oral history projects, either completed or ongoing, based on the demonstrated influences of the communities involved and associated issues, approaches, and methodologies. The importance of images for immigrant narrators and practical methods on how to use images are included. This book also includes a chapter which gives a step-by-step *summary* on how to plan and complete an oral history project. Another chapter has a case study of an individual life story. Practical templates can be found in the appendices. My experiences as an Australian oral historian, following internationally recognised standards of best oral history practice, transfer to any English-speaking country with immigrant people who want their stories recorded.

Acknowledgements

Thank you to the following people who, without their contributions and support, this book would not have been written. Huge thanks go to American oral historian and Left Coast editor, Nancy MacKay. Nancy inspired me to write this book, and then gave timely and kind reassurance and expert guidance. Huge thanks as well to Dr Paula Hamilton, Australian oral historian, public historian, and professor of history, who kindly offered expert advice. I also want to thank Australian and American oral history colleagues who advised and assisted with ideas and case studies. Thank you for sharing your expertise in oral history, descriptions of your own oral history projects, and for freely giving your time to the project: from Australia, Sandra Blamey, Frances Rush, Leonard Janiszewski, Effy Alexakis, and Denise Phillips; and from the United States, Vicki Albu, Roy Chan, and Anne Huang. Thanks go as well to the kind people who provided photographs, acknowledged in situ. I also deeply appreciate the help of Gaye Doran, Adult Second Languages teacher and refugee advocate and activist, for her profound insights into the difficulties of being a refugee. Jenny Grey, an Australian Migrant Services Manager, similarly gave me insight into the lives of immigrant people. I am indebted to Judy McLean for sharing her extensive knowledge of English grammar. I want to thank and honour all the narrators I have interviewed over the years, especially immigrant narrators, for all that they have taught me about recording personal histories. Thank you to my wonderful adult students at Sutherland TAFE, who inspired me to become an oral historian. Thank you especially to the narrators who have kindly allowed me to write about them in this book. My most special and loving thanks go to my family, who always gave positive encouragement. Lastly, thank you with love to my husband, Dr Mark McKirdy, who painstakingly read the manuscript and offered excellent suggestions. Without the efforts of these people, the completion of this book would not have been possible.

Chapter 1

INTRODUCTION TO ORAL HISTORY

"What people will do for freedom."[1]

Anna was an eyewitness to the first student demonstrations in Hungary that led to the widespread revolt against Soviet control in 1956. Soon after, in December, she and her husband John decided that they wanted to live in an egalitarian country. They escaped to Austria in disguise and with the unanticipated help of an opportunistic people smuggler—a man they think was probably a train conductor. Anna and John waited on Budapest's main railway station for about eight hours for a train. John, in his early twenties, was dressed as an old man and acted the part, stooped and shivering. Anna played the role of a young girl waiting with him. Had the ruse been discovered, John would have been shot dead on the spot. He had no identifying papers; the identity book that all Hungarian people over the age of fourteen had to carry at all times was with the army. At that time young Hungarian men did obligatory army service for the Soviet regime in the Hungarian army, and identity papers were kept until release but John, on the last day of a leave break, had no intention of returning. Anna would have been sent to prison. The people smuggler, who helped them cross the border into Austria after taking all their savings, was shot dead.[2]

Tina was a barge kiddie living on a Dutch barge, which her family realised was intended for use by Hitler for his foiled invasion of Britain in World War II. Barge kiddies were the children of barge owners. They traditionally attended boarding schools throughout Holland because of their lack of a fixed address; the barges navigated Holland's extensive canal systems. Dutch boarding schools

Practicing Oral History with Immigrant Narrators by Carol McKirdy, pp. 13–20.

closed during the war or were used as barracks, so Tina lived on her father's barge and missed school almost entirely. Her narrative describes what it was like to be a child living in an occupied country during World War II. She remembers asking her mother where all the people with the stars had gone. As a small child she gradually realised that she saw the numbers of Jewish people, identified by yellow cloth stars, decrease in Holland. At the time Tina and her mother did not know why. She also recounted amusing stories. The family's barge once hit a bridge and started leaking. According to Tina, her father used the traditional method of Dutch barge drivers to fix the hole; he jammed it closed with a lump of bacon, purposely kept for such an emergency. Tina and her siblings used to ask if they could eat the bacon, but their mother always said, "No, that's for the barge . . . when we spring a leak."[3]

Rachel described life as a child in Kakuma refugee camp in Kenya, Africa. When talking about meals, she perfunctorily explained that there was no breakfast or lunch but sometimes they had dinner. A terrible lack of food was stated honestly and succinctly as an everyday fact of life.[4]

Luigi, an Italian immigrant, joined hundreds of builders working on the construction of the Sydney Opera House, now a world famous building. He warmly remembered regular meetings with the Opera House designer, Jørn Utzon. Jørn Utzon, an iconic and internationally acclaimed architect, not only took the time to chat with ordinary workers, he could speak the multiple languages of the worksite's multicultural workforce. Perhaps Luigi's oral history is the only personal record of this fact. Luigi also worked on the construction of The Snowy Mountains Scheme, the largest engineering project ever undertaken in Australia and one of the most complex hydro-electric schemes in the world.[5] Construction began in 1949 and lasted for twenty-five years. Sir Robert Menzies served as Australia's prime minister for eighteen collective years, including a number of years during the scheme's construction. Prime Minister Menzies visited the site and spoke to the workers, but Luigi's understanding of English at that time was so limited he didn't realise he was listening to Australia's leader. As a new arrival in Sydney, Luigi found Australia very different from Italy; despite these differences, he enjoyed his new life. When Luigi arrived in the 1950s, Australian hotels, the easiest place to buy alcoholic drinks, shut at 6 P.M.[6] Luigi recalled that in Italy, places that sold alcohol stayed open until the early hours of the morning. Luigi used to be baffled by the actions of his Australian workmates and friends who, after finishing work at 5 P.M., went to as many hotels as they could, to buy as many beers as they could carry, when hotel closing time drew near.[7]

Rosalin's mother, describing life in Malta immediately after World War II, told her daughter, "Malta never fed us." Rosalin said the nutritional quality of her food was so poor her naturally curly hair turned straight. Each meal consisted of bread soaked with olive oil and spread with tomato paste. Rosalin still finds this delicious. The education system in Malta at that time was rudimentary and even more so for Rosalin because she was a girl. As Rosalin could not attend school she amused herself. One of her favourite games was playing in a nearby cemetery, jumping from grave to grave. Her highly superstitious mother not only had to worry about how to feed her family, she was also genuinely terrified ghosts would haunt the family because of the disrespectful behavior of her daughter.[8]

Bob, an immigrant from the United Kingdom, recalled in precise detail his time spent in the British Navy during World War II. When war broke out he was too young to enlist, so he altered his birth certificate using Indian ink, cochineal, and an eraser. His Aunt Mary helped him and then avoided the wrath of the family by moving away and joining the Women's Royal Naval Service. Bob and Mary made such a good forgery that his "new" birth date affected all subsequent identification documents. Bob's meticulous recall of his war years included Rest and Recreation leave spent with Australian Navy sailors on tiny islands in the Indian Ocean. They played beach cricket together, and Bob remembered that "England always won." This is an intriguing *memory* in the context of the long-term, fierce but friendly cricket rivalry between Bob's home country and the nation of which he became a citizen.[9]

What Is Oral History?

Oral history is a collaborative creation between a narrator, often referred to as an *interviewee*, and an interviewer. A knowledgeable narrator shares memories with an interviewer who has carefully researched and planned the interview. Oral history is a highly effective method for gathering historical information that gives a personal perspective of what happened in the past and that also adds to and supports what we know from mainstream, traditional history compiled from primary, secondary, and tertiary sources. Oral history is sometimes described as a means to fill in the gaps, and it does so by adding individual recollections of the past that are interesting, informative, enlightening, and sometimes extraordinary to listen to. Often the best way to find out about the past is to ask someone who was there and experienced it or who knows about it because of knowledge passed down.

Oral history records unique life memories. The history is told, recorded, and kept for future generations. Carefully prepared interviewers support narrators to retell recollections, memories, and subjective perspectives of what happened in the past so that these versions are recorded for posterity. Interviews typically follow a question and answer format responsive and sensitive to the narrator's dialogue so that a comprehensive narrative record is created. The process of collecting oral history results in lasting first-person records. The entire process is carried out following nationally and internationally endorsed ethical guidelines which protect participants, such as those of the American Oral History Association and Oral History Australia.[10]

The focus of an oral history project can vary enormously. Interview content is dependent on the context and purpose of the overall project or single interview, the narrator, and the narrator's knowledge and experiences. Is an individual life story being collected? The narrative may centre on family or community groups. Is the purpose to create a record of cultural traditions? Will the project be a museum exhibition? A narrator may have first-hand knowledge of historical events. The oral history may be about a particular place or location and the associated narratives. There are numerous possibilities. Every oral history creates a new record and this might be an entirely new aspect of the period. Oral history complements existing *historical records* and gives a sense of the subjectivity of historical experience. It helps our desire and need for finding consistent historical truth, for finding out what happened in the past as clearly and honestly as possible. Oral history narratives can be mapped by fact-finding to support known and established historical truths such as dates, names, and locations. An oral historian is always mindful to confirm the narrative according to established factual, historical background such as dates, facts, documents, and figures. Oral histories may be analyzed, but this is not mandatory; sometimes the recording is done purely and simply to create a record so that memories are not forgotten, which is often the case for family oral histories.

It is preferable that interviews are digitally recorded; *analog* methods can of course be used, but have largely been superseded, have limited longevity, and are difficult to process and archive. Ultimately, the most important factor in oral history is the narrative. The audio interviews are supported with written record keeping such as field notes, logs, summaries, and *transcripts*. Oral history is published in a variety of ways for all sorts of audiences. Secure storage practices are implemented so that the valuable memories are kept safe. Oral histories are archived because of their historical value and for accessibility. Although oral histories may be recorded purely as audio records, they can be valuable narratives for research purposes.

Oral history is a powerful method of recording history, especially individual life stories and recollections. History is much more than dates, facts, documents, and figures. Oral history narrative helps fill in historical detail by adding interest about everyday life, personal viewpoints, and memories of history that would otherwise not be recorded and retained. People speak for themselves and talk about what it was like to be there, why they behaved as they did, and also their feelings and responses to life in the past. Recalling the past helps narrators—and in turn, their listeners—to make sense and meaning out of what happened in the past.

Voices, accents, vocabularies, local word usage, and individual expressions and sayings are conserved. Oral history is a relatively easy way for a narrator to record memories, as it is far less daunting and time-consuming than the creation of a written account. It may be the sole way a particular aspect of history is recorded. Limitations of oral history can apply to traditional history; for example, a narrator's version of events has individual bias and may have errors. The same applies to traditional historical records. Oral history gives a voice to all sections of society, including people not always considered in traditional historical record keeping, such as ordinary people and those in marginalised groups who know the history because they experienced it.

Recording history using the spoken memories of people has been an enduring pursuit of humanity. Oral evidence has been the main way people have passed down history. Printed written history is relatively new, and its use varies according to when a culture acquired writing. Oral history is important; memories recorded are lives and experiences continued and remembered. Traditional history is a written record to support a specific historical narrative, created from primary, secondary, and tertiary sources. Interestingly, in traditional history a *primary source* can be a person with direct knowledge of a situation such as an oral history narrator. As with history in general, oral history can be entertaining as well as historically illuminating, but the difference with an oral recount is that the history is personalised and is designed to be listened to. Listening to a narrator tell a story with the accompanying vocal tone, accent, pronunciation, inflections, and nuances of speech is wonderful; the appeal of listening to and learning from a significant and real story is generally appreciated and valued. Most people love listening to stories, especially those that are true, unique, and personal. Oral history speaks to us.

History has been documented orally since ancient times. The practice of telling a story has been around for thousands of years. Spoken narratives were passed down from generation to generation preserving collective memory. Australian indigenous people have told their stories orally for generations. "It is through oral communication that concepts and beliefs about The Dreaming[11] are passed on from one generation to the next. They help us to understand about the past, present and future. Oral traditions include the use of storytelling, song, dance, art, craft making, giving instructions and directions. All of these forms of Oral Traditions help to pass on specific cultural practices and values, language and laws, histories and family relationships."[12] Many cultures throughout the world use *oral traditions* for remembering the past—for example, Aboriginal societies in North America.[13]

For some cultures a writing system didn't exist. Worldwide, written history is a relatively new phenomenon for the vast majority of people, as know-how and technology that supports literacy development was previously unfamiliar. The printing press wasn't invented until the eleventh century in China and the fifteenth century in Europe. Access to written material was not prevalent until modern times, and in the past the ability to read and write was not universal. In most countries high literacy rates are a comparatively recent situation. Current World Bank data shows that even today, the adult (15+) literacy rate for people who can, with understanding, read and write a short, simple statement on everyday life remains very low in many parts of the world.[14]

In our *digital* era, recording narrative orally follows the example of prior generations and cultures and remains an apt method for recording history. Oral history is individual and confined, but the record of the past gathered in an oral history interview helps bring the wider history of a shared past vividly to life. For the benefit of our shared future, oral history is a wonderful way to commemorate ordinary lives.

Immigration

The United Nations estimated that in 2013 there were almost 232 million international migrants. Scientists have identified that migration has been a consistent feature of human behavior. "Historical migration of human populations begins with the movement of *Homo erectus* out of Africa across Eurasia about 1.75 million years ago."[15] There are numerous theories about why modern migration occurs, including Neoclassical economic theory, Relative deprivation theory, World systems theory, Climate cycles theory, Buffer theory, and Lee's Laws, among many others. The various theories show that people migrate for numerous reasons. Ultimately it depends on the circumstances of both the home and adopted country. Migration may be forced or voluntary. Lee's Laws classify reasons for migration into two groups:

push and pull factors. Push factors are things that are unfavourable about the place someone lives in, and pull factors attract people to another area. Push factors include not enough jobs, few opportunities, inadequate conditions, desertification, famine or drought, political fear or persecution, slavery or forced labour, poor medical care, loss of wealth, natural disasters, death threats, desire for more political or religious freedom, pollution, poor housing, landlord/tenant issues, bullying, discrimination, poor chances of marrying, condemned housing, and war. Lee's pull factors are: job opportunities, better living conditions, the feeling of having more political and/or religious freedom, enjoyment, education, better medical care, attractive climates, security, family links, industry, and better chances of marrying.[16]

Like many countries Australia and the United States have large migrant populations.[17] Australia's expansion and development is synonymous with migration; migration is an integral aspect of Australia's identity. In Australia, unless you have indigenous heritage, your forebears were relatively recent migrants. Indigenous Australians living in Australia for an estimated 60,000 years were subjected to the arrival of around 80,000 mostly petty criminals, known as convicts, from 1788 to 1840 as a result of British government policy. At that time, Australia was used by the British Empire, in effect, as a giant and distant jail. Free immigrants came as well, all initially from the United Kingdom. Successive migration has seen groups of people move to Australia from all over the world at various times for various reasons, adapted and shaped by each home country's situation and in response to Australia's needs and policies and, currently, changes brought about by internationalisation. After World War II most Australians shared the view that Australia had to "populate or perish," an expression that summarized the belief that if Australia did not increase its population, it wouldn't survive as a nation. Since World War II over 6.5 million migrants have moved to Australia.[18] Australian migrants are encouraged to keep their cultural identity, language, traditions, and religious beliefs while accepting Australian laws and systems.

Immigration is sometimes controversial because "it can impact on the character of a society quite rapidly, creating anxiety among those who do not want change. While much public policy is made as though only numbers and skills matter, in the political arena these are often given much less prominence than national issues—the race, religion, languages and 'culture' of those who are being admitted."[19] Oral history interviewers work with individual narrators and personal history, but an awareness of underlying national immigration facts, attitudes, policies, and historical context is essential background knowledge for projects recording the narratives of immigrant narrators.

Conducting an oral history project is a rewarding professional activity for both novice and experienced oral historians. Facilitating the recollection and articulation of a narrator's story is significant because it introduces unknown history and brings a new perspective to known history.

Chapter 2

WORKING WITH THE IMMIGRANT COMMUNITY

"We really have appreciated their input into our community."[1]

Oral history immigrant community projects, like any oral history project, can vary enormously. Regardless of whether the project has just one narrator or many narrators, the ultimate success of the project relies on practical, informed, and cooperative community and individual engagement, support, consultation, and planning with the immigrant community. A real understanding of the community is essential; otherwise, the interviewer will not know what to ask.

What Is Meant by an "Immigrant Community"?

We all belong to ethnic, cultural, spiritual, and linguistic groups, of which the basis could be a racial, social, geographic, or historical relationship. In Australia "ethnic" has popularly been used to refer to people from non-English-speaking backgrounds or with non-Anglo–Celtic origins.[2]

The Importance of Getting Support in the Immigrant Community

Engaging support from the immigrant community that is the focus of the project is vital. Without the support and backing of the community, whatever the cultural background, the oral history project may unintentionally reflect the oral history project designer/interviewer's preconceived perceptions and interpretations of history that are important to a community rather than

Practicing Oral History with Immigrant Narrators by Carol McKirdy, pp. 21–47.

what the community thinks is significant, relevant, and should be recorded. Also, without immigrant community endorsement the project may struggle to be viable because of a lack of practical support, interest, and commitment from the people who are supposedly recording their histories. With immigrant community oral history projects, *ownership* of the project should come from the immigrant community. The oral historian's primary role is to help make the project a reality. In helping the project come to fruition, there are opportunities for the oral historian and the immigrant community to jointly consult and guide, creating a mutually beneficial exchange of ideas.

Stories and storytelling are important to people; they are integral to any community. A well-considered and planned oral history project supports individuals or communities to tell their histories and to preserve them so that what happened to people within a distinctive community is not forgotten. Recording oral history can be particularly important for immigrant communities because in telling what has happened in the past, information is encapsulated and preserved that allows a community to explore and expose issues, problems, and concerns from the past and of living in a different country. Important information about what has happened to community members, descriptions of events, difficulties and hardships, joys and triumphs, and accounts by the narrator of the "who, what, where, when, why, and how" of the past are passed on by the narrator to listeners who can then acknowledge and better understand a collective past. Recording an immigrant community's history is not simply a matter of creating a record; it is a means for people within the community to clarify and illuminate the past to build community self-esteem and confidence.

Immigrant Historical Narrative

When immigrant histories are recorded, community members have access to recalled memories which enable them to interpret their unique historical situations. A community benefits from keeping a historical record of significant events. Children benefit in particular. Creating an oral history of parental experiences supports children and grandchildren in understanding their family's background and provides validation of past experiences for parents and elders. Stories help people to understand community adaptation to a new culture and way of life. Stories of course can be—and are—passed down without the structure imposed by an oral history project. The advantage of a formal project, which can be summarized as a carefully planned and researched interview with audio and/or *video* records and associated written records, associated images, archiving, and an array of publication options, is that the narrators' voices are enabled to tell and preserve history indefinitely. "Oral history is commonly accepted as an excellent methodology for recording unique history. Recorded oral histories provide access to social groups that are under-represented in documentary archives and illuminate intimate lives and subjectivity."[3]

Immigrant Oral History Project Ownership

Within the contextual background of any immigrant oral history project should be the understanding that the best means to engage a community is for the desire and need to conduct an oral history project to stem from within the immigrant community itself as opposed to from a relative outsider to the community. Without this project structure there is the danger that outsiders, who may have the very best of intentions, may not become attuned to how a particular immigrant community functions. For an immigrant oral history project to succeed, there has to be an awareness of cultural nuances. Going in as an outsider oral historian can create cultural landmines, annoyance, may possibly appear condescending, and is especially awkward if an oral historian carelessly "barges in" on a tight-knit community. If outsiders go in without a welcome, it is much more challenging to get people committed to a project; the support of a community is essential.

Establishing Cooperative Contacts within the Immigrant Community

Establishing friendly and useful contacts within an immigrant community is essential. Find people who can help you. In any community, including immigrant communities, there are usually natural community "ambassadors," leaders, and representatives who are very aware of what is going on in their community; they can help enormously as facilitators and networkers. They will know who should definitely be interviewed and who might have specific information or could give leads to follow for further interviews. They will know how, when, and where to approach people, inappropriate times of the year for interviewing, and so on, and can act as go-betweens. Community insider helpers will assist the oral history project to build community bonds and trust. Endorsed community leaders can play a similar role; it depends on the immigrant group. Without community connections and support, narrators might not be cooperative; they might, for example, not turn up to interviews or make the interviewer very aware that the project has low priority, and may show minimal interest or not tell their history authentically. The project may not be advertised appropriately or receive negligible or token promotion. Locating people who can assist will vary depending on the community group. It is easier in communities which have formalised designated leaders. It is more difficult to locate informal leaders who, for example, can't be looked up in a phone book, but a community representative may be asked for this information.

Committees

Establishing an oral history committee is an excellent way to establish parameters for the oral history project and to authenticate and advertise it. A committee can help connect community members to the project as well as provide organizational structure. A committee also provides opportunities to acknowledge and validate the roles of community helpers. Having a committee may help support funding applications, because a committee's structure implies and imposes a verifiable structure of governance and therefore a means for a funding body to monitor grant implementation.

The Role of an Oral Historian in the Immigrant Community

In many respects an oral historian who is not a member of the immigrant community being documented is an outsider, but there is a place where the oral historian can fit in. Working as an outsider is not a barrier; sensitive community engagement is effective. Developing a partnership aiming towards common concepts and project goals is productive. Cooperation is most effective when a community desires to record its history but lacks the ability to execute a project. An immigrant community group that has the desire to record its history may not have the means to implement the project, and a partnership with an oral historian with the associated technical, digital, writing, and organizational skills works very effectively. Immigrant community groups differ, but for some, professional or relatively high-level English writing skills are an asset because they enable the immigrant group to clearly and effectively publish their history in the language of their adopted country as well as, if wanted, in a familiar language. An immigrant narrator's written vocabulary may be adequate for daily life skills writing such as filling in forms, writing short texts such as notes, and expressing familiar, predictable personal narratives, but for a true reflection of the past the narrator may have insufficient skill to express nuance and complex thoughts.

Publishing the Narratives—Consider Potential Consequences

Oral history and storytelling projects are personal recounts; if published beyond transcripts, *CDs*, or *DVDs*, and *repository* storage, the testimony becomes public. Narrators should know exactly what the consequences are if their testimony or parts of it are to be made public. Very specifically, they should be made fully aware of what it means for them if their testimony or parts of it are published digitally, for example, on a website or on a social utility such as Facebook. This is even more important when a narrator's English language understanding isn't perfect or because of limited exposure to digital environments and implications.

As with any oral history project, it is essential that the oral historian takes care with people's feelings and circumstances. If the intention of the oral history project is to publish to a wide audience, this is very important. Excerpts from the narrations, chosen by the project team or oral historian to publish in a radio show, video, within a digital story, in a book, and so on may not be the choice of the narrator as "the best or most significant bit."

It's important at the outset of the oral history process to let narrators know what will happen with and to their recorded interview. A one-and-a-half hour interview intended to be part of a radio show could easily be reduced to less than ten minutes for broadcast time. Narrators should receive very clear written and spoken explanations for the publication process of the interviews in the project. They should also be made aware that their words may not be published in any manner apart from in *archives* for general distribution and research.

Perhaps the most helpful way to learn about best practice for engaging the immigrant community in an oral history project is to look at a selection of oral history project examples from Australia and the United States that have engaged with immigrant communities meaningfully, productively, and appropriately.

Sudanese People in the Sutherland Shire—A Moving Community, Sydney, NSW, Australia

Sudanese People in the Sutherland Shire—A Moving Community Oral History Project recorded local Sudanese immigration history by recording the narratives of recently arrived Sudanese refugees and citizens and people in the community who assisted them to settle. The Sutherland Shire is a district in Sydney, NSW, Australia. A relatively small but significant number of about seventy-five Sudanese people made the Sutherland Shire their home after leaving Sudan.

Figure 2.1: Friends at the launch of Sudanese People in the Sutherland Shire—A Moving Community Oral History Project, Sutherland, NSW, 2010. Photo courtesy Mark McKirdy.

"From the mid-1990s to late 2005, over 16,000 Sudanese came to Australia under [Australia's] humanitarian resettlement program, 4,500 as refugees."[4] An oral history record of local Sudanese people and the combined efforts of local residents who helped them to settle in the Sutherland Shire was established to help people understand more about the Sudanese living alongside them, demonstrate how refugees settle, and show the help and services available in the area for new settlers. As a community it was decided that to keep a historical record of significant events in the community was important.

Oral histories were recorded of people from the Sudanese community and people who assisted them from a local church, Caringbah Anglican Church; a regional state government support service, Gymea Community Aid Information Service Incorporated (GCAIS); local government, Sutherland Shire Council; and a tertiary training organization, TAFE (Technical and Further Education) NSW Sutherland College. The oral history project recorded Australian

Sudanese immigrant community history and recollections of life in Africa, the Dinka language, and images. The project was funded by the Australian Government Department of Immigration & Citizenship, The Refugee Council of Australia, and Tradies, a local recreational club with a strong tradition of providing monetary and in kind support for local community groups. Gymea Community Aid and Information Services Incorporated launched the project at Sutherland Library, a large central library, in Refugee Week, 2011. The launch was the culmination of the yearlong oral history project. The project had the full support of the local Sudanese community. The local and NSW Sudanese leader and spokesperson at that time, Mr Ajang Deng Biar, was involved in negotiations from the outset, was on the project committee, and was also a narrator. Mr Biar's family was the first Sudanese family to move into the Sutherland Shire. I served as project oral historian. As a Sutherland TAFE teacher I had informed links with the community through teaching Sudanese people in Language and Literacy classes. The other committee member was the Migrant Services manager of GCAIS, Jenny Grey, who had extensive connections with the community, especially for helping settlement in Australia. Unusually, the idea for the project came initially from me as the oral historian rather than the Sudanese community, but Mr Biar supported the project as a cooperative venture. One of my students was helped to write a story about life in Africa, and the short recount was word processed. Reaction to the typed recount was enlightening and touching; when given the typed story, my student held it close and said repeatedly, "my story." Seeing firsthand the significance and effect of having a tangibly presented personal recollection of an aspect of the past motivated me to see if other people in the Sudanese community wanted their histories recorded.

Project Aims

The oral history project's aims were comprehensive. They included:

- support the community's understanding of cultural diversity
- foster preservation of immigrant community history
- build the capacity of the community to understand the unique circumstances of Sudanese people
- reduce racism and break down barriers through building awareness and understanding of people who were new settlers and appeared different
- enable second-generation Sudanese children to gain knowledge and understanding of family history

- build unique, Australian History curriculum-relevant educational resources (the oral histories were also published and linked on Australian educational websites)
- record for posterity the type of support services operating in the community and provide models for future citizens
- encourage community participation of newly arrived migrants
- foster social inclusion and community harmony

The oral history project was seen as a means to help immigrant refugee families who needed support, as settlement in a new country is a time of great stress. Additionally, a lack of understanding of parental traditional culture could have potentially created intergenerational conflict. Creating an oral history of parental experiences supported children in understanding their parents' background whilst everyone in the family adapted to a new culture. The project was seen as a means to provide validation of past experiences for parents, and it supported understanding of community history in Australia. It provided insights into the circumstances which led people from Sudan to call Australia home and their unique stories about the experiences of being a refugee in the Sutherland Shire.

Involving Sudanese Children

An important aspect of the project was the inclusion of testimony from Sudanese children. Children do not usually narrate for oral history projects because of limited life experience, but the local Sudanese children experienced significant and uncommon childhood events and had valuable contributions to make because of their unique understanding and experiences. The short recordings they made speak of history from a child's viewpoint; for example, a teenager retold her family's story of when she was a child, narrowly avoiding bullets while driving across a bridge to an airport after her family left Kakuma Refugee Camp in Kenya, Africa, to come to Australia. As she was an infant at the time, the story was not her own recollection, but it became one of her stories because it was an important story retold by her family. Two primary/grade school-age brothers retold a family story of loss about a pet goat and a cat with nine kittens.[5]

To collect their stories, five Sudanese children participated in a version of Vox Pops (Vox Populi).[6] Short interviews about their African stories were recorded as they played during a break from study at a community homework club. For the Vox Pop recordings, they were asked two questions: What is the best thing about living in the Sutherland Shire, and what is your favourite family story from Africa? The committee set up to establish the project, especially the Migrant Services manager and the Sudanese leader, wanted Sudanese children to be involved in the overall project. In addition to the interviews, a national radio presenter who volunteered his time taught the children the fundamentals of using a digital SLR camera, *microphones*, and field audio digital recorders. The children also experimented with interviewing each other—lots of fun! The Sudanese children, as well as others who chose to observe rather than participate, gained insights into the process adult members of their community, mostly relatives, were experiencing.

The oral history project's title is indicative of the circumstances of Sutherland Shire's Sudanese residents. Their oral testimonies were poignant in their retelling of their diasporic and frequently traumatic lives as they moved around Sudan seeking safety and freedom from conflict, then to Kakuma, a northern Kenyan refugee camp, and then finally to Australia and within Australia as they sought to establish new and viable places to live ordinary lives in peace.

Background to the Project

The Sutherland Shire is a designated Refugee Welcome Zone; a Local Government Area which has made a commitment in spirit to welcoming refugees into the community, upholding the human rights of refugees, demonstrating compassion for refugees, and enhancing cultural and religious diversity in the community. The community as a whole was notable in the manner in which it embraced and supported Sudanese people settling in the area. Church, community support services, local government, and TAFE worked together and individually to assist Sudanese people settling in the area. The Sudanese people who moved to the area were mainly humanitarian refugees from Sudan's south. They were a unique group in the local community because of their refugee status and the terrible circumstances they endured in Sudan through African diaspora, civil unrest, and conflict before arrival in Australia. The premise behind the oral history project was that the Sudanese histories should not be forgotten and left untold. The experiences of the Sudanese refugees would add to the knowledge society has about people living through terrible circumstances and the challenges and opportunities of living in a new country and community—for them, the Sutherland Shire. Sudanese men, women, and children were deemed the main beneficiaries of recording the histories as well as being the catalyst for the project. People in the Sutherland Shire who supported the Sudanese refugees to adjust to a new life in the community had their stories recorded as well. They benefitted too because their contributions were acknowledged and recognised, and a record was made for future, similar events and opportunities to assist community groups experiencing similar situations. In effect it was anticipated that the entire community would benefit because people could gain insights into the backgrounds of their Sudanese neighbours and local support procedures and systems. The oral history audio files were organised into a *collection* and published online.

Recording the stories orally was an ideal historical collection method. Many of the Sudanese people did not express confidence in their ability to record their histories in writing. As people who had experienced African diaspora, most of the narrators had limited access to educational opportunities in Africa in their first language, let alone the opportunity to gain English writing skills at the appropriate level. As well, the focus of the Sudanese community was settlement in a new country, which included the myriad and exhausting demands on their time of starting afresh in Australia. Having an oral historian recording their history was not unduly time-consuming or impositional for narrators, including those who had excellent writing skills. Also, in Southern Sudanese culture, oral tradition is very strong.[7] Twenty-two interviews were recorded in total and over half of the narrators were Sudanese.

Engaging the Sudanese Community

"Ownership" of "Sudanese People in the Sutherland Shire—A Moving Community Oral History Project" belonged to local Sudanese people. Without support for the project from the Sudanese community it is doubtful that the project would have succeeded. Meetings with Mr Biar made this very clear. The local Migrant Services Manager, Jenny Grey, who worked closely with all the immigrant communities in the Sutherland Shire, also required that the Sudanese community had to give the project full approbation. Having the imprimatur of the Sudanese community made the following possible: finding narrators, three of whom were interviewed with an interpreter; following leads for further interviews; sourcing supporting material such as photographs and authentic South Sudanese African music; having constructive discussions regarding the project and its goals; and staging a large community launch event attended by many Sudanese people not directly connected to the project.

Early Romanian Immigration to Minnesota Oral History Project, Minnesota, United States

The purpose of the Early Romanian Immigration to Minnesota Oral History Project was to record and preserve knowledge of the ways in which Romanian immigrants came to Minnesota and how the valuable *cultural heritage* of the Romanian-American community has been preserved in Minnesota, a state in America's Midwest. The oral history project organisers were aware that very little historical information on the topic of Romanian immigration to Minnesota was documented, even though Minnesota is home to 6,300 people of Romanian ancestry. Romanian-American immigration peaked in Minnesota in the 1920s. There was a resurgence in immigration from Romania to the United States as a result of the Romanian Revolution of 1989 and after the fall of European communism at the end of the 1980s.[8]

The goal of the project was to record ten oral histories to provide an archive of unique Romanian-American immigration to Minnesota stories during 1900–1940. Interviews were conducted as video oral histories in the spring of 2013. Eleven interviews were actually recorded. The interviews have been archived for public access by historians, researchers, and other interested parties, firstly as typed verbatim transcripts archived at the *local history* museum. For the longer term and greater public accessibility to the recorded histories, the project team made a video documentary based on the experiences of early Romanian immigrants to Minnesota entitled *A Thousand Dollars and Back.*[9]

HORA—Heritage Organization of Romanian Americans

The commissioning group for the project was HORA—the Heritage Organization of Romanian Americans. HORA was awarded a Legacy Grant from the State of Minnesota Arts and Cultural Heritage Fund to conduct the oral history project. The state of Minnesota created the tax-supported fund for local history projects. Partners in the project were the grant applicant, Heritage Organization of Romanian Americans in Minnesota (HORA), and also the Romanian Genealogy Society (RGS) and Town Square Television (TST). Town Square Television is the local community cable TV station serving the seven cities of Northern Dakota County in Minnesota. A second grant enabled the involvement of Town Square Television, adding an exciting element to the oral history project because of TST's expertise in creating television documentaries and videos. Production of the video, based on the oral histories, increased the capacity to give the project a wide audience and provided

Figure 2.2: John H. Sarafolean, a narrator for the Early Romanian Immigration to Minnesota Oral History Project. South St Paul, Minnesota, 2014. Photo courtesy John H. Sarafolean.

an appealing way for people to learn about early Minnesota Romanian immigration history. The project team felt that watching a documentary would bring the histories to life and be more educational, interesting, and entertaining than reading transcripts.

Figure 2.3: Sofie Petrascu Sarafolean, John Sarafolean's paternal grandmother with two of her children (1888–1981). Circa 1920. Photo courtesy John H. Sarafolean.

The Project Team

Project team members, led by Vicki Albu, had Romanian heritage and also included the executive director of Town Square Television. They selected narrators based on their level of firsthand knowledge of Romanian immigration to Minnesota and their direct experiences with the preservation of Romanian cultural heritage. Vicki Albu conducted the interviews in English. When a narrator was asked to share Romanian language examples, Vicki was assisted by trained volunteers who spoke Romanian. The project designers found that they

Figure 2.4: John H. Sarafolean's Uncle Pete (centre) going fishing. South St Paul, Minnesota, Circa 1930s. Photo courtesy John H. Sarafolean.

did not have to specifically cater for Romanian narrators who were not confident English speakers because all the narrators spoke English fluently. The project team had planned to have native Romanian-speaking facilitators present during all the interviews, but second language assistants were not necessary at any stage of the project. Nor did the English proficiency of narrators unduly affect written documentation based on the interviews. Producing transcripts based on the interviews was, in the case of a few narrators, slightly challenging because of a narrator's strong Romanian accent. This slightly increased the cost of transcription services, but it was not considered a major issue.

Engaging the Romanian Community

The steps taken to engage the Romanian community and get their support for the project were straightforward. The oral historians working on the project were fortunate because two active Romanian-American organizations in Minnesota gave the project excellent support: the commissioning group, Heritage Organization of Romanian Americans in Minnesota, founded in 2009; and the Romanian Genealogy Society, founded in 2011. Both organizations helped the implementers of the project to identify potential narrators. Integral to the project's success was that key people involved with the project were of Romanian descent, and this assisted the project to become a reality because of intense personal interest, commitment, background understanding, and Romanian cultural knowledge. Vicki Albu, the project manager, has Romanian heritage, but as a child was not really aware that she was a fourth-generation Romanian-American. She had a great desire to know more about her Romanian great-grandfather and his history. She discovered that there was a scarcity of historical information on Romanian-American immigration history, specifically in relation to Minnesotan history. This led to her interest in the history of Romanian people who chose to immigrate to America and especially Minnesota. She felt the best way to amass historical data was by collecting the stories of people who had firsthand knowledge of the historical experience and era. Raluca Octav, historian, key project team member, and a person with strong connections and involvement in the Minnesotan Romanian community, grew up in Romania before immigrating to the United States in 1991; she was personally able to identify with the narrator experiences.

The non-Romanian background community in Minnesota was not initially directly involved, but through the Minnesota Legacy Grant process the project workers were able to bring the project to the attention of the broader Minnesota community with displays, marketing, and ultimately the video documentary, which had a premiere to which all the community was invited. The consultation and planning process evolved over a long period. The historical research for the project was carried out over many years preceding the actual interview project. The Minnesota Historical Society, the agency that administered the Legacy Grants (funded by a portion of sales tax paid by Minnesotans), also referred the project designers to Barb Sommer, a U.S.-based oral history expert who provided training and guidance to the project team. As the project was funded by a Minnesota Legacy Grant, the project scope was necessarily limited to Romanian immigrant experiences in Minnesota, so Romanian people from other parts of the United States did not participate.

Outcomes of the Project

The expected outcomes of gathering the oral histories were validated using performance measures including the number of interviews successfully completed and deposited, along with transcripts, at the Dakota County Historical Society in South St. Paul, Minnesota. The goal was for ten subjects with 60 to 90 minutes of finished raw video each, totalling up to fifteen hours of video. Progress had to be measured at least quarterly and reported to the grantor as required. Researchers and the public had to have future access to the oral histories at the Dakota County Historical Society library and museum in South St. Paul, Minnesota. A plan was made to offer video *files* and transcripts to the Minnesota Historical Society and to the University of Minnesota's Immigration History Research Center.

The issues explored in the interviews were wide-ranging. In addition to telling their families' immigration stories, the narrators were asked to share examples of ways in which they personally preserve Romanian culture and tradition. Questions explored included:

Why did your family choose to come to Minnesota?

What route did your family travel while immigrating?

What family connections existed?

What differences existed between your homeland in Romania and your new residence?

Show and tell us about your cultural traditions, folk costumes, and recipes.

What religious beliefs or organizations influenced the family?

What jobs did you have in Romania and in the United States?

What were your experiences in assimilating to a new lifestyle?

What do you think defines a "Romanian-American"?

Did you or any family members go back to Romania?

Can you show any historical photos or memorabilia (documents, folk costumes, heirlooms) that relate to your family's immigration experience and arrival in Minnesota?

Can you show or describe a cultural tradition that exists in your family (music, dance, cooking, winemaking . . .)?

The project team aimed to gather firsthand recollections of unique experiences of Romanian-American immigrants to Minnesota between the years of approximately 1900–1940. There were no direct cultural barriers encountered during the interviews except for a few situations where the narrators discussed events in Romania outside of the scope of the project and for which the interviewer was not fully conversant because the topics were outside the research preparation scope. However, an important aspect of the project was the project team's awareness of the typically sociable and gregarious nature of the Minnesotan Romanian community in general, and they took this into account with the people who were interviewed. Because of the anticipated sociability, they made sure that the narrators felt very comfortable and relaxed prior to the on-camera interviews. The interviewer took the time to ensure a social connection was established before engaging in the formalities of the interview process.

"In Their Own Image: Greek-Australians" National Project, Australia

"In Their Own Image: Greek-Australians" National Project began in 1982. This large, multifaceted, and comprehensive project has a substantial oral history component of over 2,000 recorded Greek-Australian oral history interviews. The project, and its commitment to undertaking oral history, is ongoing. It researches the historical and contemporary Greek-Australian presence in Australia and overseas. It aims to provide a wide-ranging and detailed social, cultural, and historical image of Greek-Australians. The project, as well as collecting a substantial and significant oral, literary, and visual archive,

Figure 2.5: Bill Florence (Vasilios Florias) being welcomed to Australia, Melbourne, Vic., 1922. Photo courtesy S. Raftopoulos and J. Florence, from the "In Their Own Image: Greek-Australians" National Project Archives, Macquarie University.

Figure 2.6: Greek National Day celebrations, Sydney Opera House, Sydney, NSW, 1984. Photo by Effy Alexakis, from the "In Their Own Image: Greek-Australians" National Project Archives, Macquarie University.

has produced various publications including books linked to major sociocultural history exhibitions that have toured nationally and internationally; has undertaken film documentaries, multimedia presentations, a televised film documentary about the project, and various historical documentary videos; and has assisted in supporting future generations of Australian and international historians and sociologists by providing resources for both university teaching and research into Greek-Australian and migration history. The project's diversity enables wide audience appeal. One of the primary aims of the project is to acknowledge the fascinating, significant, and substantial contribution of Greek migrants to Australian society. The history of Greek-Australian voices and material culture from almost two centuries of Hellenic presence in Australia is documented. Previous to the project's implementation, recorded Greek-Australian history was insignificantly archived.

"In Their Own Image: Greek-Australians" National Project was started by Sydney-based documentary photographer Effy Alexakis. Leonard Janiszewski joined the project in 1983 as a historian of Australia's social and cultural past. Both continue as the project's curators. Effy and Leonard recognised that Australian national and state archives, libraries, and museums did not collect nor recognise the significance and contributions of Greek-Australians to Australia's cultural diversity and history. They found this applied to other ethnically and culturally diverse groups living in Australia as well. "As a result, groups from non-English speaking backgrounds have been effectively alienated, marginalised, and left broadly unacknowledged in the symbols and pre-eminent events and developments of Australia's history—a myopic, monocultural vision of British-Australia prevails." Janiszewski and Alexakis realised as well that "socio-cultural historical material in languages other than English in Australia's national and state repositories is poor in both overall amount and applied significance, a situation also reflected in the scarcity of professional Australian historians and heritage specialists with linguistic skills in a language or languages other than English."[10]

"In Their Own Image: Greek-Australians" National Project: A Cooperative Endeavour

"In Their Own Image: Greek-Australians" National Project moved into a new phase in 2001 when it became a cooperative project, with the establishment of university ties allowing the history of the Greek community to be explored within a university museum and scholarly research context. The wider Australian community benefits; by focussing on the history of an ethnic community, cross-cultural influences upon the development of mainstream Australian culture and history can be explored. The partnership involves Macquarie University in Sydney, working in association with the Australian History Museum and the Discipline of Modern History.

The project is reliant upon its strong ties and relationship with the Greek-Australian community. Liaison, connection, and communication with Greek people as well as approval by Greek-Australians form the cornerstone of the project. The title of the project is significant; "In Their Own Image" ensures and confirms that the focus of collection for oral history narratives and associated images, memorabilia, and documents reflects how Greek-Australians see themselves and the ways they want their histories recorded. Material that is gathered is of specific importance to Greek-Australians. Engagement with the broader Australian and international community occurs through outreach activities arising from this relationship via the collaborative touring exhibitions and museum displays, public lectures by prominent Greek-Australians, teaching videos for both public and institutional use, and web access via the institutions that have held their exhibitions.

Engagement with the Greek Community

Narratives of Greek-Australians recorded in audio or video and an archive of family snapshots, letters, diaries, private official papers, and memorabilia from the homes of Greek-Australians living in Australia and overseas have been created. The key to success when engaging with Greek-Australian community members is personal contact. Effy and Leonard work personally and directly with and among their subject, the Greek-Australian community. The traditional institutional attitude of engaging the community via publicity campaigns and waiting for narrators to respond was not followed in favour of personal and individual communication.

Oral History Interviews

At the outset, the historical and contemporary presence of Greek settlement in Australia was geographically identified in each state and territory utilising existing primary and *secondary source* material. Primary sources included: colonial and Australian census records, including a 1916 secret census of Greek people; early newspapers; police reports; government gazettes; significant documentary photographic collections; and historical diaries and journals. Secondary sources included historical and sociological research articles, university theses, and national and state listings of official Greek Orthodox communities and regional associations. Field trips throughout Australia were made to locations identified as having potential narrators and research material. Field trips have also been made to Greece, Cyprus, Egypt, and Fiji. Field trips to the United States were carried out because of the substantial sociocultural influence of Greek migration from the United States to Australia.

Oral history interviews follow recognised, strict methodological and documentation practices, including *legal release* for use in research, publication, electronic transmission, and exhibition display. Effy and Leonard do all the interviews. Effy interviews in Greek and most of Leonard's interviews are conducted in English. They are both present for every interview. One person does the interview, and the other person creates field notes to assist transcription. Effy photographs narrators after the interview because by this stage narrators feel comfortable with their presence and intentions. Most of the interviews are audio recordings. Some are also recorded as digital videos, for the purposes of film documentaries. Effy and Leonard find that video recording can be far more intimidating than audio recording for some narrators, so suitability for the medium is assessed before the interview.

Narrator Question Themes

The oral history interviews consistently include the following broad thematic areas: life in country of origin, reasons for migration and settlement, initial settlement experiences, occupations, racism, family life, social activities, language problems, education, cultural identity, attitude toward host society, gender and generational differences, cultural maintenance, and considerations of re-migration. The oral histories are comprehensive, based on inquiry into the thematic elements of each narrator's individual experience. People who wanted to participate in the project with written rather than oral responses were assisted to do so with the help of a prepared questionnaire. Diversity of narrators is considered essential within the project, particularly regarding age, experiences, outlook, occupations, and period of migration or the number of generations removed from an original Greek forebear. Effy and Leonard were conscious of the need to create a comprehensive and indicative collection of Greek-Australian narratives. Early interviews recorded on analog tapes are *digitized* to ensure preservation and accessibility. Most interviews were recorded in English, with a small number in Greek. Detailed outlines of the interviews are logged in field notebooks. Creating transcriptions of the interviews is an ongoing process.

Interview and Associated Materials Collection Processes

Narrators are photographed and sometimes filmed in their work, home, or social environments. Historical family photographs, private papers, and memorabilia are sensitively selected, then copied or donated for inclusion in the project's collection. The selection process includes an evaluation of an item's state of preservation; its historical, sociological, or cultural significance within both a Greek-Australian and broader Australian community context; its common or rare status; its highlighting of the narrator's story; as well as whether it can be easily utilised for research and display. Identification details of all items are cross-checked through available sources, and the personal significance of each one to its owner, or owners, is meticulously recorded. All documentary information gathered is systematically placed in a database, an ongoing process so that individuals and families, themes, particular types of items, photographic subjects, and migration and settlement periods can be accessed, assessed, and cross-referenced quickly for research purposes leading to publication or museum exhibition display. All physical items undergo preservation procedures and cataloguing.

Exhibitions created by the project are used to attract new research material from the general public. Individuals, families, and organizations have been prompted to provide the project with fresh primary resources and personal insights. Major exhibitions based on the narratives and associated resources include: *In Their Own Image: Greek-Australians*, Mavri Xenitia: *Black Foreign Land, In Her Own Image: Greek-Australian Women—A Historical and Contemporary Insight*, and *Selling an American Dream: Australia's Greek Café*.

"Selling an American Dream: Australia's Greek Café" "research focuses on the Australian Greek café's key role in the Americanisation of Australian popular culture (eating and socio-cultural habits) from the start of the twentieth century—a 'Trojan Horse' selling the 'American Dream' to Australians. It directly challenges the accepted monocultural perception of popular culture in Australia during the twentieth century, and, furthermore, (Australia's) historical socio-cultural relationship with Greece, the United States and even Great Britain and New Zealand . . . Re-interpretation of Australia's past can only succeed in raising ethnic history from the marginalised ghetto onto the larger national, and indeed, international stage—an epic, transnational history is steadily emerging."[11]

Greek cafés were the social centre of hundreds of Australian towns from the 1900s to the late 1960s. Rather than selling Greek food, the cafés sold American-style drinks such as milkshakes and sodas, ice cream and candy, and plain Australian food. They were regarded as exotic and glamorous, with the sights, sounds, and tastes of America. The cafés had names such as The Californian, The Niagara, and Monterey Café. They were beautifully designed with American architectural influences and often had jukeboxes. They were sometimes positioned near movie theatres ("the pictures") and this consolidated the idea of escapism. Rural Australian people loved the cafés because they were open long hours, from early morning to late at night, were inexpensive, and offered great service along with the experience of participating in American culture. Greek-Australian migrants had connections with Greek migrants to the United States and implemented methods and equipment from America.[12]

This particular aspect of "In Their Own Image: Greek-Australians" National Project preserves important history, as narrator Peter Martin explains: "The Greek café was part of the identity and social fabric of the community.

Every time we lose a Greek café we lose part of the history, part of our memory, part of our sense of town and region."[13]

Oakland Chinatown Oral History Project, Oakland, California, United States

The Oakland Chinatown Oral History Project (OCOHP)[14] is a place-based storytelling project that documents the living history of Oakland Chinatown through interviews and photography.

The project's mission is to capture and preserve the living history of Oakland Chinatown by facilitating an ongoing community dialogue across generations and cultures. As well as being intergenerational, the project is multiphase and long-term to comprehensively enable the collection and preservation of the ongoing narrative of community life in Oakland Chinatown. Previously, Oakland Chinatown's oral history was not formally documented; much of its history was stored in the minds of the community's elders. The motivation behind the project is that some of the early, otherwise forgotten history of Oakland Chinatown resides in the memory of community elders and should be collected for future generations before it is lost. As older generations die, so do

Figure 2.7: Oakland Asian Cultural Center Tai Chi group enjoying an outdoor exhibit, Madison Park, Oakland, California, 2012. Photo courtesy Oakland Asian Cultural Center.

their stories and their knowledge of local history and practice. As well, personal experiences, lessons learned, and the struggles and successes of growing and developing Oakland's immigrant community should be told for posterity. The Oakland Chinatown Oral History Project is focused on telling and preserving the narratives of the Asian community of Oakland Chinatown, but the project's website allows people from all over the world to access the stories.

Oakland is the third largest city in the San Francisco Bay area and a major California port. OCOHP began in 2006, is ongoing, and is in its sixth phase. The project has also incorporated eleven interviews conducted by high school students in 1997. The students interviewed Oakland Asian community elders about their memories of Oakland Chinatown during World War II through the 1960s. Further intergenerational interviews were conducted in 2007 and then transcribed in 2008. The project entered its digital archive phase in 2009.

In 2014, the Oakland Chinatown Oral History Project started documenting the living history of the Asian Branch Library, housed in Oakland's Pacific Renaissance Plaza, through interviews of longtime branch advocates, librarians, and patrons, spanning five decades. The Asian Branch Library in Oakland Chinatown is the busiest branch in Oakland's library system. It is remarkable among library branches throughout the United States in that it houses collections in eight different Asian languages: Chinese, Japanese, Korean, Vietnamese, Khmer, Lao, Tagalog, and Thai. The Asian language collection reflects the diverse Asian immigrant population living in Oakland now and during the last several decades. The Asian Branch Library is an important and integral part of Oakland Asian community life and serves as a meeting place offering important opportunities for cultural and social exchange within the diverse immigrant community. Oakland Asian citizens of all ages and circumstances make use of the various opportunities to participate in community activities offered at the library. By capturing the stories of library patrons it is anticipated that not only will a history of the library be created but also a history of the Asian community patrons who use the library.

Engaging the Asian Community

The Oakland Chinatown community formed a Community Advisory Committee and developed a community history project during the 1980s. Research from this was developed into a book.[15] In 2005, a few of the members of this group and other Asian community members approached the Oakland Asian Cultural Center to create an oral history project. Since OCOHP began in 2006, the community advisory committee has overseen the development of themes for each phase of the project. The committee works to ensure the project's process is community-based and includes local residents, scholars, and past youth and elder participants. Within the contextual background of the Oakland Chinatown Oral History Project is the premise that the best way to engage the community in an oral history project is for the desire and need to collect oral history to come from within the immigrant community itself. Oral historian Angela Zusman served as project manager, and another oral historian, Nancy MacKay, serves on the project's advisory committee and assists with consultation and planning. As well, she trained the project managers and volunteers in correct oral history techniques and archiving.

The Oakland Chinatown Oral History Project enables Oakland's younger generations to have meaningful dialogue with older generations in their community. Residents feel a sense of ownership and an understanding of the historical context of their community. Oakland's Asian community is more informed and they have the capacity to be active citizens in the public decision making processes of the project.

The Interviews

With narrators, the project explored issues relating to discrimination, displacement, culturally significant place-making, family ties, the use of public and private space, and the environment. Specifically, information was gathered about narrator experiences of detention during immigration; the personal impact of the 1882 Chinese Exclusion Act, introduced to stop Chinese immigration; and unequal treatment of immigrants based on nationality. Where possible, OCOHP wanted to record dates of important community historical events and collate a collection of old photographs of Oakland Chinatown places and people. The project also explored people's emotions. For narrators who were not confident English speakers, Cantonese translators were used. As is usual when translation services are used, additional time and effort were required during interviews and later for the subtitling of videos and exhibits. When sourcing narrators, OCOHP found that many elders felt their life stories or daily life experiences were nothing special and often did not understand why their stories needed to be told. They also had to be mindful of the cultural differences between the various Asian immigrant groups and their relationship histories as different communities.

The commissioning group for OCOHP is Oakland Asian Cultural Center, located in Oakland. The project receives foundation grants seasonally along with individual donations to help support each phase of the project.

"From Afghanistan to Australia: An Oral History Study of the Experiences of Loss and Hope among Hazara Refugees," Australia

"From Afghanistan to Australia: An Oral History Study of the Experiences of Loss and Hope among Hazara Refugees" is documented in a PhD thesis being undertaken at the University of New England, NSW, Australia. The interviews and associated PhD thesis are the work of Denise Phillips, a University Medal recipient.

The "Hazaras are the third largest ethnic group in Afghanistan."[16] They live mainly in central Afghanistan and make up between nine and nineteen percent of the population.[17] Their first language is Hazaragi or Dari. Suffering persecution, "The Hazaras have been the targets of multiple documented massacres and human rights abuses at the hands of Taliban forces."[18]

Historically in Australia, the vast majority of asylum seekers who have reached Australia by boat have been officially recognised as refugees. As of June 2012, 10.3 percent of humanitarian visas granted in Australia in 2011–2012 were to people born in Afghanistan. The statistics do not identify ethnicity; however, "the overwhelming majority of Afghan people recently arriving by boat have been Hazara." About 10,000 Hazara people live in Australia.[19]

Denise explains her work:

> The project uses oral history to record, present and analyse the experiences of loss and hope among Hazara refugees living in Australia. Hazaras are a persecuted ethnic, Shiite minority from Afghanistan, and they make up significant numbers of the asylum seekers who have arrived by boat since 1999. The study draws on interviews conducted over a decade with unauthorised boat arrivals and entrants selected under Australia's Humanitarian program. The thesis has two key tasks. Through in-depth case studies, it explores the significance of each story and the layers of meaning which the narrator gives to his or her experiences. In listening to the Hazaras' personal dreams and private suffering, it uncovers the way hopes for safety are often juxtaposed against a continuing grief within resettlement over the loss of loved ones and their homeland.
>
> Secondly, the thesis discusses the methodological and ethical practices used when interviewing Hazaras and shares the process of becoming more adaptive within cross-cultural settings. It examines the way personal interactions and the narratives are shaped by bereavement, trauma, crises of uncertainty, and varying circumstances determined by government policies. The thesis builds

on earlier research which examined the tensions between remembering and forgetting: some Hazara narrators drew on a persecuted identity and Afghanistan's founding violence to make sense of present suffering, while also silencing or forgetting other experiences in order to exercise agency or coping mechanisms within resettlement.[20]

The project is remarkable in its execution. Although the project is ultimately designed for academia, it demonstrates the potential of oral history. The interview method is deeply compassionate to people who have suffered enormous loss and trauma in both the recent and deep past and, also for some, loss of hope for a positive future. Listening to Denise speak with great kindness to deeply sad narrators demonstrates that oral history is not simply limited to fact-finding; it can also be a very humane approach to interacting with someone who has information to share and record. The project also demonstrates how a lack of language competence should not be a deterrent to gathering narratives. "I'm 21 and have no any happy days"[21] and "To dream my family tonight"[22] are perfectly understandable sentences despite imperfect English syntax. The project also demonstrates how an oral history project with its associated comprehensive research can be used as a means to attempt to inform public and government awareness, based on identified facts. Denise challenged the Australian government on policy regarding Afghani asylum claims, saying, "The Labor government's justification for its suspension policy cannot be sustained against the overwhelming evidence of a worsening crisis in Afghanistan."[23]

Chapter 3

TRAUMA

"You can never really understand what they went through
. . . he showed me bullet holes, scars left by bullet holes . . .
the car was ambushed, everybody was killed except him,
they thought he was dead, but he was just left there to die."[1]

Distressing, Heartbreaking Narratives in Immigrant Oral Histories—Traumatic Narrative, Implications for the Narrator and the Interviewer

Interviewing people who have experienced and witnessed traumatic, terrible events and awful situations and who have suffered great sadness and grief requires additional thoughtfulness, sensitivity, and understanding from the interviewer. Immigrant narrators, because of their often unhappy and challenging immigrant status and displacement, may be more likely than usual to have stories that are distressing to tell and listen to. In an interview context where the narrative is traumatic, both the narrator and the interviewer must take extra care. The narrator may be negatively affected by retelling personal traumatic narrative, and the interviewer may be negatively affected by hearing the narrator's story.

The implications and difficulties of collecting traumatic narrative are compounded when a narrator finds communicating in English difficult.

An immigrant narrator with a background that is traumatic is not, by default, traumatised. Vulnerability cannot be presumed. Experiencing traumatic events does not necessarily lead to lasting emotional and psychological damage. Some people recover relatively unhurt from tragic and shocking experiences, others do not; personal resilience, an individual's capacity to adapt and cope with adversity, differs.[2] The Australian Centre for Posttraumatic Mental Health guidelines emphasise that the majority of people exposed to trauma do not go on to develop distressing conditions in response to a traumatic event.[3] As well, a narrator may have received professional psychological treatment that equipped them to deal with traumatic experiences. However, oral history interviewers must be especially prepared when they interview someone with a potentially harrowing background, because there is a possibility that trauma will be a facet of the interview process.

What Is Trauma?

The American Psychological Association defines trauma as an emotional response to a terrible event like an accident, rape, or natural disaster. Immediately after the event, shock and denial are typical. Long-term reactions include unpredictable emotions, flashbacks, strained relationships, and even physical symptoms like headaches or nausea. While these feelings are normal, some people have difficulty moving on with their lives.[4]

The Australian Centre for Posttraumatic Mental Health explains that any event that involves exposure to actual or threatened death, serious injury, or sexual violence has the potential to be traumatic.[5]

The American Psychiatric Association specifically defines a trauma as direct personal experience of an event that involves actual or threatened death or serious injury, or other threat to one's physical integrity; or witnessing an event that involves death, injury, or a threat to the physical integrity of another person; or learning about unexpected or violent death, serious harm, or threat of death or injury experienced by a family member or other close associate. . . . The person's response to the event must involve intense fear, helplessness, or horror.[6]

The psychological, physical, and social effects of trauma are varied, distressing, and difficult. Sufferers can experience flashbacks, shame, helplessness, anxiety, depression, terrifying memories, nightmares, defensive emotional numbing and disconnection, and extreme fear. Social consequences include trouble with functioning in the community, at home, and at work. People who were traumatised can experience related physical ailments such as chronic pain or heart problems, or be generally unwell.

Someone may have a traumatised background and then find that immigration to a new country is traumatic because of the move from one set of circumstances to another. People who experienced enormous hardship and anguish in their home country may find life remains very difficult. Everyday life is altered—new language and/or accents, food, housing, transport systems, shops, government, jurisdiction and administration systems, schooling methods, lack of family and familiar friends, different weather, animals—the list is seemingly endless. People may never have used an automatic teller machine, used a pay phone, turned on a light switch, or put a key in a lock. Typical donations of flat pack furniture are baffling for people who have never built self-assembly fixtures. Change can be traumatic; in reality, trauma is not limited to precursor dangerous events such as war, catastrophic events, or torture. Gaye Doran, an Adult Second Languages teacher and refugee supporter and advocate, has also observed the trauma and guilt Sudanese refugees experience in Australia simply because they are in Australia while relatives and friends remain in refugee camps or in perilous conditions in South Sudan. Sudanese relatives living in Australia are well aware of the situation of their loved ones because they have personally experienced the traumatic circumstances. As well as trauma caused by the guilt of feeling, for instance, safe, secure, well-fed, and adequately housed, adjusting to new ways of living are extremely difficult, and the loss of a different way of life compounds the problems experienced. Job credentials do not necessarily transfer from one country to another; people used to living communally are separated into different suburb and town locations, and there is the constant difficulty and worry of trying to financially support family overseas. Sending money to family overseas is very hard because of the expense of starting afresh in Australia.[7] Adjustments to new ways of living are very stressful.

Psychologists sometimes make a distinction between "simple" and "complex" trauma. Simple trauma relates to a distinct, one-off traumatic event. Complex trauma refers to trauma that is sustained through prolonged or repeated events. Multiple traumatic events may have a cumulative effect. The impact of complex trauma might be more serious and long-lasting. Psychologists also refer to cultural trauma, which is trauma experienced by parents and that has a traumatising effect on their children.

Traumatic Memory

Traumatic memories differ from normal memories that are articulated in predictable narrative structures. Traumatic memories are often disjointed and unable to merge with memories of other experiences. The contextual information of time and place that typically characterises autobiographical episode memory is absent, and the memories may be fragmented.[8]

Traumatic memory may be very clear and vivid. Ben Morris, a participant interviewer of Australian Vietnam War Veterans from 2 Platoon, Alpha Company, Second Battalion, Royal Australian Regiment (2RAR) in Vietnam, 1967, recalled with great clarity an extremely distressing and traumatic incident in which 2RAR, a platoon he commanded, was involved. Four Vietnamese civilians were accidently killed by members of his platoon. Media reports and historical records unfairly describe the event as a massacre and atrocity and are highly critical. Official war records were validated against war veteran accounts in an effort to establish and present truth, reality, and a correct record of why and how the tragedy occurred. Eighteen of the thirty-three soldiers in the platoon were interviewed in order to gather eyewitness accounts. Ben remembered the ambush vividly as did most of the men he interviewed. "The moment between the machine gun firing on the civilians and hearing the whimpering of children caught in the gunfire was very short but still remains with us all."[9]

Cautionary Ethical Strategies for Oral History Interviews Dealing with Trauma

Set Professional Parameters before the Interview

The oral history project should be well conducted with a professional structure and format and with a strong ethical regard for the welfare of the narrator. Establish clear boundaries between the narrator and the interviewer so that you are able to conduct the oral history project interview effectively and objectively while listening empathetically and with due regard for the emotional well-being of the narrator and yourself as interviewer.

Oral history interviews that have traumatic content require a caring environment; participating in the interview process may be therapeutic for the narrator, but the oral history interview environment is informed, caring, considerate, and compassionate as opposed to therapeutic in the professional sense. Trauma issues can appear unexpectedly in any oral history interview and it is important to be prepared to allow for professional counselling support for any narrator if needed. Expert counsellors help people to understand their feelings and support them to manage their reactions to trauma to help them regain control of their lives. An oral historian collects and records historical information based on a planned interview. The oral historian records unique life experience that helps people to work with and understand, organise, present, and interpret the past. Oral historians might engage with people who have traumatic memories, and they do so in an ethical framework, but they are not therapists.

Of course, there is always the possibility that the interviewer is both an oral historian and works in the field of psychotherapy.

As the oral historian, you may be the only person who has taken the time to listen attentively and sensitively to the narrator's story. Narrators who have experienced trauma have not necessarily sought help to talk about their experiences with counsellors, psychologists, psychotherapists, psychiatrists, or trusted friends or supporters. This could easily be the case for a narrator with less-than-perfect English and living in a new country, because additional effort is required to source the help. In any oral history interview, a bond often builds between the narrator and the interviewer. This, of course, helps to build rapport within the interview and adds to its veracity. The oral history interview bond is not necessarily a bond that leads to an ongoing friendship, companionship, social interaction, and support outside of the interview, but it may; as human beings we make friends and connections in many circumstances. Where trauma and its effects are apparent, the interviewer may find that a sociable, caring, and supportive bond created through an oral history interview is insufficient for the emotional and psychological needs of a narrator who has experienced trauma. The narrator may need more than friendly support. In everyday life we are familiar with the practice of "accidental counselling": people who find themselves supporting others seeking advice and guidance, often about extremely significant issues. An oral history interview can compound the practice of accidental counselling because the interview is usually very revealing, in-depth, and personal. However, the needs of the narrator might best be met by some form of professional support, which the interviewer has a duty of care to ensure is available if need be.

Consider the Possible Need for Counselling

The cost of professional counselling in its various forms may be prohibitive for the narrator. In Australia there are superb services, often at no or minimal cost, provided by organizations such as beyondblue, STARTTS, and Lifeline.[10] Religious organizations of all denominations may offer support, as do community organizations and settlement programs set up specifically for migrants and culturally specific groups. Immigrant narrators may have trusted elders and community members who offer support. Narrators with connections to government educational providers such as TAFE NSW [11] have free access to qualified psychologists if they are students or planning to study. The narrator can also be advised to visit a doctor. Advice should be culturally appropriate, but also be mindful that a narrator may, for various reasons, not want to access traditional support agencies or networks offered within a cultural community because of privacy concerns. Usually, counselling services are multilingual, enabling non-English speakers to speak about their problems in a familiar language. beyondblue advises that "providing support doesn't have to be complicated. It often involves small things like spending time together, having a cup of tea, chatting about day to day life or giving the person a hug."[12] Megg Kelham conducted the Bereaved by Suicide Audio Project for the Mental Health Association of Central Australia. Megg realised the importance of preparing both the interviewer and narrator. "I did not protect myself properly during this project. In the future I will begin all my interviews with some lightly chatty questions focussed on what the interviewee plans to do when the interview is over. I will also carefully consider and share my own post interview activities. In trauma interviews this could include . . . coffee with a friend, going to the movies or getting some formal counselling. There are so many simple but important ways to prepare the interviewer and the interviewee for the emotion and memory creating journey that an oral history interview is."[13]

Conduct Thorough Research and Be Well Prepared

Strengthen your awareness of the narrator's prior situation with thorough research of the background and circumstances behind the narrator's story. If you are interviewing a war veteran or refugee, for example, find out as much as possible about the conflict or diaspora period: dates; nationalities affected by the situation; the political, social, cultural, and religious background; and knowledge of the geography and physical conditions, such as the food, education, medical, and housing conditions of the narrator. Respect narrators by taking the time to do research; they want to tell their narratives without having to explain conditional facts and figures or sense from your questioning that you are unaware of the publicly known background to their stories. Having general background information is essential; however, it's important to be a careful listener to the firsthand story of the narrator without imparting the impression that you already know what they are going to say. Furthermore, one of oral history's greatest strengths is that it adds personal perspective to historical facts, so it's important to not get preoccupied with fact-finding at the expense of listening to the narrator and responding accordingly. Additionally, as the interviewer, it's also important to remember that you might be collecting history that has not yet been documented or offers a different understanding to information previously gathered. Preconceptions can be problematic and may affect the quality of the interview. As well, be cautious when researching. The sanctioned *public history* of the narrator's country may be inconsistent with the historical experiences of the narrator, especially someone who experienced traumatic events because of a political, social, or religious view or ethnic background that was violently or strenuously opposed. This is especially relevant for a narrator who belonged to a vanquished or escaping group. The past, as documented to be remembered for the public history of the victors, may be recalled very differently by the narrator. Terrible events the narrator remembers may have been officially justified, sanitised, or "forgotten" in mainstream historical records.

Denise Phillips, an Australian oral historian, interviewed Hazara refugees who came as asylum seekers from Afghanistan to live in Queensland, Australia.[14] Through her interviews with Hazara men, she studied the impact of subjectivity when using memory as an historical source. The trauma her narrators experienced was compounded by the terrible history of Afghanistan. Stories passed down of atrocities that happened in the past complicated and exacerbated recent traumata. Her interpretations of the oral histories she collected built on the concept of "wounded memory" by French philosopher Paul Ricoeur. Ricoeur contended that a country with a history established through violence creates "wounded memory" where past grievances take over and other experiences are forgotten. Historical trauma and enmity through generations may be relevant for many narrators and countries.

Sir Winston Churchill won the Nobel Prize for Literature in 1953 for his six-volume history of World War II. As Prime Minister of the United Kingdom for most of World War II from 1940 to 1945, he is widely regarded as one of the great wartime leaders of the twentieth century. He is, however, quoted as saying that history is written by the victors and "History will be kind to me for I intend to write it."[15]

Usually I am thoroughly prepared for my interviews, but on one occasion I unexpectedly had the opportunity to interview Rachael, a young woman who had spent most of her childhood in Kakuma refugee camp in Kenya, Africa. I was conducting another, planned interview, and Rachael was visiting my targeted narrator and presented me with an opportunity to record her story. In her interview Rachael described the harsh living conditions of the camp, including highly irregular meals and infrequent food supplies. When I asked if her family could have obtained additional food by gardening, hunting, or fishing, she became frustrated and annoyed with me because it was obvious that I was unaware of the physical limitations of living in Kenya's Turkana District's semi-arid desert environment of dust storms, minimal natural water supply, and scrub vegetation, and also of living in the highly structured Kakuma camp environment. As Rachael explained, at Kakuma you had to live in the designated area for your group, for example, refugees from specific areas such as South Sudan, Rwanda, or Eritrea. People were not physically confined, but they stayed in their identified areas. Rachael's interview was part of a series of interviews for Sudanese refugees.[16] My interview with Rachael was unanticipated and fortuitous, and I'm glad I took the opportunity to record her experiences even though research of the living conditions at Kakuma had not been necessary at that stage of the oral history project. My question about sourcing food was reasonable because I was aware that in some refugee camps refugees grow and catch food and establish shops, but for Rachael's situation in Kakuma this was not the case.

Interviewer Behavior during the Interview

Be aware of, and follow the lead of narrators' agendas; whatever the reason, they are giving their narratives despite the difficulties of telling their stories. Professionally set boundaries will enable a narrator to tell the story with an interviewer who is capable of listening and responding in a manner that allows the interview to be carried out productively and with the focus on the narrator. An overly emotional reaction by the interviewer to a distressing recount, such as crying or a strident expression of outrage, is likely to upset the narrator and affect the flow of the interview, disrupt the interview, or stop it.

Be careful about, and aware of, your own emotional situation; unresolved or pertinent personal issues may impact on the narrator-interviewer relationship and the manner in which you respond to the narrator's story. Empathy for someone's pain or suffering affects people in different ways. Always remember that the focus of the interview is the narrator. If you think the narrator's story will unduly upset you, ask a colleague to do the interview because you may not be able to cope. In International Relations Specialist Denise Leith's fictional short story based on the experiences of an Australian asylum seeker who lived in a Sydney detention centre, the asylum seeker explains: "It's hard for people to hear because they're too afraid to even begin imagining what it must be like"[17]

Create a Safe Atmosphere to Support the Interview Process

Create a safe atmosphere for the interview by listening empathetically with understanding and warmth and by being well prepared; the narrator should feel protected and secure as the story is divulged. Listen carefully to what the narrator knows rather than what you want to know. Don't lose concentration. Most oral historians are aware of momentary lapses of concentration for all sorts of reasons: unanticipated external noise that may affect the sound quality of the recording, the awareness that a battery is faltering, making a mental note to follow a lead, and so on. Gadi BenEzer, intercultural psychologist, academic, and author, says that a person recounting trauma needs to sense that full attention is being paid to the recounting of the story, because the person feels enwrapped in the traumatic experience and senses that outsiders can't understand the situation.[18] If the oral history project has multiple interviews, treat and respect each narrator as an individual. Narrators may have a common background, but their personal stories are unique; especially when the experiences involve trauma, individuality must be acknowledged. If you are working with an interpreter, ensure that the interpreter is fully informed and prepared.

Be culturally aware. Find out how you should refer to the dead, for example. The interviewer's cultural mores are not necessarily those of the narrator. Listen carefully and be conscious of your own responses. Be careful about your body language and facial expressions that may influence the narrator as the story is told.

Follow accepted practices of prior non-recorded meetings by phone and/or or in person to get to know the narrator beforehand. Face-to-face pre-interviews are invariably better for narrators who have difficult testimony to impart, because they allow more opportunity to establish a relationship; this is particularly important for narrators who find speaking in English by phone frustrating. Talking about the proposed interview gives the narrator a chance to become mentally and emotionally prepared and to start reflecting. As well, there is time ahead of the interview to establish the physical setting for the interview and to sort out possible logistical difficulties for the interview beforehand. For example, it may not be possible to record in a quiet environment, interview time may be limited or difficult to schedule, or the narrator may want to confirm the interview project arrangements with family and community members.

Structure the interview, as is customary, with initial "easier" factual information-gathering and lead-in questions. Sensitivity may, however, be required at the very start of the interview, as genealogical information about parental details, for example, may cause grief because they involve loss and death. Questions about when and where the narrator was born and lived may elicit sad responses for homelands that may be gone forever. Many of my adult students who grew up in Yugoslavia in Southeast Europe hated the fact that the place and name they called home as a child no longer existed on maps after 1991. They were saddened to refer to the country in which they were born and raised as Former Yugoslavia rather than Yugoslavia.

Be flexible and responsive to working on gaining trust. You may need to prove your genuine interest when listening to a narrator's story. Sticking rigidly to commonly established methods of good interview practice might be inappropriate. If the narrator wants to sit on the floor or a couch rather than at a table set up in the accepted manner, bend the "rules." Adjust the positioning of the recording equipment accordingly. Put the needs of the narrator ahead of good interview practice and techniques if necessary. The narrator's story and emotional well-being are the most important concerns.

Through recounting, the narrator may be in a vulnerable situation, and the interviewer has to consider the narrator's mental and emotional welfare. Conducting an interview may bring back prior trauma, and the narrator suffers anew. As interviewer, you become a witness through listening to what was experienced and endured. As with any interview, allow the narrator to own the interview, and give the narrator the understanding that they are allowed to take the time to be silent, including extensive periods of silence, and the time to articulate difficult memories and proceed at the narrator's own pace. An oral historian's carefully planned interview should not cause harm. If the narrator seems to be emotionally at risk, don't record the narrative. However, give the narrator the opportunity to tell the story at a later time as, presumably, in physically presenting for the interview, the narrator does indeed want to tell the story.

Don't deny what the narrator says or argue with them about what they say because it seems too awful to believe or differs from other accounts for the period. When Savan Hin told me that she knew the sclera of the eyes of the Khmer Rouge members who ate body parts of their victims turned red,[19] I was tempted to ask, "Are you sure?" I didn't. I was aware from other historical accounts[20] that cannibalism was practised by some Khmer Rouge members. My thoughts as I listened to Savan and her description about eye colour as a result of anthropophagy were uncertain, but for Savan this particular occurrence was very real. Scientific researchers may, indeed, have identified this phenomenon amongst cannibals. For Savan, red, bloodshot eyes were not only a certainty; describing them seemed a means to illustrate and confirm the awfulness of people who ate their compatriots. "Anyone dismissing oral history because the narrators detail some mythical explanations may be discarding some good primary source material."[21]

Don't be tempted to blame narrators for the trauma they experienced or in any way be judgmental about their experiences.

Make sure support for the narrator is available if needed. Savan, who survived living in Cambodia under Pol Pot's rule, had easy access to free professional counselling with a qualified psychologist, including, if wanted, an interpreter or bilingual psychologist. She could also seek help from church parishioners, including church professionals experienced and trained in offering counsel, and family and friends she could talk with. Savan did not access any support that I suggested, because she was at peace with what she had experienced. Savan expressed a feeling of closure because of her Christian beliefs. To allay my concerns for her welfare, she took the time and effort to express her thoughts in writing about why she felt at ease about her experiences and why she never worried or thought about her terrible past.

Gadi BenEzer, in "Trauma Signals in Life Stories," analyzed the narratives of forty-five young Ethiopian Jews who migrated by foot to Israel from 1977–1985. He described their exodus as highly traumatic and dangerous, and about one fifth of them died. Every family involved in the journey was affected by death. The trauma experienced was both shared and individual. In his study, BenEzer identified thirteen specific signals of trauma within life story narratives. He suggests that when a narrator is recounting traumatic experiences, particular forms of expression are found in the narrative:

1. Self-report: the individual reports that a certain event was traumatic . . . an event's special painfulness, emphasizing it as being extremely distressing or wounding, or referring to its particularly negative (and/or long-term) unsettling effect on the individual

2. A "hidden" event: an event which was not narrated in the main story comes up . . . accompanied by distressing emotions such as mourning, grief, shame, or guilt

3. Long silence: a long silence occurs before or after the narration of a certain event . . . which seems to have a particularly painful or tormenting quality for the individual

4. Loss of emotional control: sudden loss of control over emotions relating to an event which is being narrated is expressed in sobbing, rage, or other responses which are uncharacteristic of this person's recounting

5. Emotional detachment or numbness: individuals report events which seem to have had a horrifying quality or horrifying consequences for

them but show no emotions during the narration. It is as if there is a forced detachment . . . isolating it from the emotional life of the individual

6. Repetitive reporting: a distressing experience is re-told in its entirety or with an extraordinary reiteration of its minute details, time and time again, as if the narrator is unable to move on

7. Losing oneself in the traumatic event: speakers seem to disappear from the reality of the interview while narrating a traumatic event. They appear to sink into themselves, submerged and overwhelmed by the event in the middle of recounting it. They may be unable to emerge without the help of the interviewer . . . as if trying to lift themselves up from a hole, maybe a mental hole they fell into via the trauma

8. Intrusive images: scenes or images of a traumatic event, or a particular fraction of it, come up involuntarily throughout the narration as quick "flashes," which clearly distract the person's train of thought and interrupt the intended flow of the narrative

9. Forceful argumentation of conduct within an event: narrators stress the reasons for their behavior within a situation instead of relating the facts, as if the traumatic quality of the event is connected to their conduct in that situation which they feel they should justify

10. Cognitive-emotional disorientation: this is characterised by a disappearance of the boundaries between the event which is being recounted and the situation of the interview

11. Inability to tell a story at all: the speaker may wish to tell the story but is unable to speak of it, getting stuck, typically, at the starting point of the narration

12. Changes in voice: the narration of trauma is often accompanied by changes in voice. The tone of the voice, its pitch, or its "colouring" will change while narrating a traumatic event

13. Changes in body language: facial expressions and body posture may also change during the recounting of a traumatic event . . . as additional nonverbal signals for detection of a traumatic event during narration.[22]

Be Prepared for Varied Narrator Reactions

Narrator reactions might seem incongruous considering the story content. Mark Klempner, an American folklorist, oral historian, and social commentator writing about Holocaust survivor interviews, described interviewing a Holocaust survivor who laughed after describing how most of her family was killed when she was seventeen, and how she described herself as lucky to have been seventeen when the tragedy occurred because at seventeen she was at an age where she was ready to leave home.[23]

Be prepared for narrators with varied emotional coping strategies. For some narrators distress will be evident to the oral historian, other narrators will not reveal their pain. Unusual laughter is one coping strategy, as is having no memory of an event, because the trauma survivor "forgets" what they endured so that they can get on with the present. A narrator may recount terrible stories in an indifferent manner in an emotionally ordinary voice that belies the narrative content. Anna, speaking about her and her husband's escape from Stalinist Hungary, sounded blasé about the fact that her young husband would have been shot dead on the spot if their subterfuge to escape had been discovered.[24] Huyen spoke enthusiastically about being a teenager in Saigon during the Vietnam War. She spoke positively about her telecommunications course and described having fun with friends. They went everywhere by bicycle. Huyen said she and her friends didn't ever think about the war; despite the closeness of the fighting, they felt safe and had no worries. She said the only thing she missed out on was going to the beach, because her parents considered the beach was too close to the fighting.[25] Rosalin recalled life as a child in Malta after World War II in a casual manner despite remembering that when she was very young there was never enough food: "Malta never fed us."[26] As I listened to Anna, Huyen, and Rosalin I empathised with their histories and the suffering behind the stories they retold, but I was bemused by how the insouciance of the recounts belied harsh and dangerous reality.

Terrence Des Pres, the late American Holocaust scholar, writer, and college professor, identified the use of laughter, humour, and comedy in various literature forms to help Holocaust survivors cope with their history of indescribable horror. He used the term "Holocaust Laughter." I want to consider the energies of laughter as a further resource. We know, to begin with, that a comic response to calamity is often more resilient, more effectively equal to terror and the sources of terror than a response that is solemn or tragic. Since the time of Hippocrates, laughter's medicinal power has been recognized and most of us would agree that humour heals.[27]

Oral historians record unique, individual history, so however narrators relay their narratives is appropriate.

After the Interview

Be mindful of how you leave the narrator at the end of the interview, physically, emotionally, and metaphorically. Wind down the interview graciously; take ample time to gently ease away from the interview's focus. Obviously, it's not appropriate to rush to another appointment. Express concerns about the narrator's well-being in response to the interview and the distressing content and issues that were discussed in the interview. Phone the following day to see if the narrator is okay and feeling comfortable with how the interview proceeded, and ask how the narrator feels. Phone again in about a week and maybe more often and ask again regarding the narrator's welfare.

The concluding stages of any oral history project, post-interview, requires contact with the narrator to confirm interview content, facts and figures, spellings, and so on. Where the narration has involved upsetting content, the oral historian should also ask about the narrator's well-being. When recording traumatic memories of South Africa's apartheid era of 1948 to 1994, American interviewer and clinical psychologist Roxsana Sussewell emphasized the importance of communicating clearly with narrators, keeping checks in place throughout, and following up on narrator welfare after the interview.[28] Henry Greenspan, in his book *On Listening to Holocaust Survivors: Beyond Testimony*,[29] strongly suggests that ongoing contact is necessary for narrators who have been interviewed regarding trauma. One interview may be insufficient and imprudent for the circumstances of the interview content and also for the narrator's overall well-being. The narrator will have time to think over what was said and prepare for the next session. Another reason for interviewing over more than one session is that being interviewed about very sad life events might be exhausting.

Closure

Oral historians are familiar with the feeling of closure, a bringing to a denouement, that an oral history interview may give any narrator. Closure is arguably more significant for a narrator who has been traumatised due to experiencing what any normal person would hate and dread to experience; a traumatised person has experienced most people's worst imaginings. Anwar's oral history focussed on her normal, happy, and peaceful childhood in Iraq and life in Iraq during the Iran-Iraq War (1980–1988) before moving to Australia with her family. The Iraq that Anwar loved as a child and the life she knew and adored was altered irrevocably by war and the dreadful effects of warfare for ordinary citizens. One day as Anwar crossed the street on an errand for her job in a bank, she thought a fly had buzzed her head. But she could smell hair burning and felt a clump of her hair drop. A bullet had skimmed through her hair and almost hit her head. On another day she was home when a bomb hit her neighbour's house. Three women were very badly hurt; they all had limbs blown off by the blast. Anwar tried to stop passing cars to take them to hospital, but people were too scared to stop. She had to get her family's gun, supplied by a citizens' defence group, to scare people into stopping so that she could organise medical support. For many years Anwar's normal life involved a litany of similar surreal activities.

At the end of the interview I thanked her as is customary, and in response she thanked me. "Thank you for your time to listen to my story . . . because I don't have anyone here . . . when I'm talking to someone . . . it helps me from inside . . . I will think about it like say another two days but at least I can tell it is something getting out of my body."[30] Anwar articulated the externalising of her suffering. She experienced a means of coping with the trauma that she experienced and the coming to terms with her awful past in order to feel more peaceful. For Anwar, retelling her story helped her capacity for emotional well-being.

Interviewer Well-Being and Reactions and Dealing with Compassion Fatigue

If, as the interviewer, you are unduly affected by an interview or series of interviews, exchange information, thoughts, and feelings with people who can validate and help you. Try to establish a support network and a community of practice with other oral historians so that you can have helpful professional conversations with people who understand your situation. Learn from other oral historians who are working in similar situations to gain expertise from them. Express your needs verbally so that you take positive action to enable you to conduct yourself usefully in interviews that recount traumatic narrative. Be cognizant of your individual emotional circumstances so that you are prepared and know how to care for your own emotional well-being.

As an interviewer you might find that you seem more affected by the recount than the narrator. "The testimony of survivors often requires a detachment that keeps them at a distance from self-pity, whereas for us the pathos of their stories, and sometimes the mere telling of such stories, is nearly over-whelming."[31]

Oral historians can learn from the experiences and practice of professionals working with people who have similar backgrounds to immigrant interviewees who want to tell their traumatic histories. The need for support for an outsider exposed to someone else's trauma is recognised in professions that regularly help people deal with trauma. For example, organizations such as Vital Hearts,[32] a United States not-for-profit organization, offer resiliency training to people who work in occupations that have interaction with traumatized people. The support offered is based on findings that involvement with someone else's trauma may have a traumatizing effect on the person who listens and helps.

Secondary or vicarious trauma can have a profound impact on professionals, creating emotional depletion, depression, anxiety, a sense of isolation or helplessness, anger, irritability, and cynicism. Without a healing response, the outcome is frequently compassion fatigue. Treating emotionally traumatized patients or clients can make huge emotional demands on those who perform these tasks. Symptoms of secondary traumatic stress disorder include such reactions as depression, anxiety, sleep disturbances, mistrust of others, isolation from family or friends, frequent or increased illness, persistent trauma imagery, and often a shift in outlook from optimism to helplessness. Many of these symptoms are similar to post-traumatic stress disorder (PTSD) and can be as damaging. Care providers incur harm across the spectrum of mental health impacts—on the emotional, cognitive, physical, relationship, and spiritual levels.[33]

Bicknell-Hentges and Lynch, professors of Counseling and Psychology at Chicago State University, writing about the cumulative trauma experienced by and reported by professionals working within the child welfare, juvenile justice, and other related mental health professions, explained: "Professionals are affected by hearing or reading histories of trauma and/or abuse. They may actually observe the physical scars of abuse. As a client talks about the trauma that s/he has experienced, internal images are created within the professional's mind and can stimulate intense feelings of compassion which can result in vicarious experiences of the actual trauma."[34]

Recording a narrator's heart-wrenching narrative places the interviewer in a position where compassion is almost certainly invoked. Compassion, or what we feel in response to another's suffering or misfortune, is our empathic distress. This is especially relevant for large-scale oral history projects focussing on an immigrant community comprising multiple interviews that have traumatic content. If oral history interviewers do not proceed carefully and with due regard for best practice when interviewing narrators who have harrowing recounts, they may experience stress because of the trauma experienced by the narrators and retold in interviews.

Chapter 4

CULTURAL AWARENESS

"The food was shocking . . . the smell . . . was something I will never forget, make you sick. I couldn't eat. . . . A chap . . . tell me what to do . . . after a few beers then you will be drunk and understand nothing. . . . so I have two schooners . . . then I start to adjust my palate."

Italian-born Luigi De Angelis described the taste of the regular, stodgy lamb meat evening meal served to resident workers on Australia's Snowy Mountains scheme and how some members of the scheme's multicultural workforce used alcohol to subvert the taste.[1]

What Is Meant by Culture?

Culture is the common expectations, values, and beliefs of a group of people, which results in culturally characteristic behaviors. Culture is made up of the mix of attitudes, customs, and principles that distinguish one group of people and the way they live from another group, or the essential way of life within a particular group. Culture is about how groups of people might behave differently when they come from socially diverse backgrounds. Cultural attitudes are learned initially within a family where language is acquired along with values, beliefs, behaviors, and ways of communicating appropriate to and valued by the family's social group. Early family values are deeply established and affect the way people behave throughout their lives. Even so, cultural beliefs, values, and behaviors are not static. People within a culture are influenced

Practicing Oral History with Immigrant Narrators by Carol McKirdy, pp. 65–73.

by people with differing cultural backgrounds encountered throughout life in numerous situations such as in daily life, school, the workplace, places of worship, within peer and interest groups, and so on. Messner further explains that attempts to define culture have three common characteristics:

1. Culture is not innate but learned, for instance, from parents, family, and social environments.
2. The various facets of culture are interrelated; for instance, it is not possible to isolate single cultural traits to identify a culture: "an Indian an Indian, an American an American, a Chinese a Chinese and a German a German."
3. Culture defines the boundaries of different groups and is shared between some individuals.[2]

Cultural Differences

Cultural differences are variations in the way of life, beliefs, traditions, and manners between different people. Different cultural circumstances can include race, class, gender, and ethnicity. Cultural differences may include differences in preferred clothing and food choices. Language can be indicative of a culture, although people who share a language do not necessarily share the same culture. Cultures can often be recognised by the principles people within the culture have to live by—the beliefs that define their particular code of conduct and values. Cultural differences identify people and give a sense of belonging. A person's culture is often extremely important and can be part of a family legacy. Culture may vary depending on location. Villagers or town dwellers, for example, might demonstrate aspects of their culture in different ways than city people. Living in another country may lead to cultural variances. Differences are not just between nations; there can be differences within much smaller and localised groups of people. Cultural difference might be influenced by the history of a region or country. Past events can influence culture. Cultural differences distinguish societies from one another.

Cultural variations in behavior are extensive. With oral history interviewing, the important consideration is to know that differences may have a bearing on the interview and to approach every interview individually rather than look for a checklist of cultural differences. "The critical requirement in successful intercultural communication is not knowledge of cultures . . . but rather, awareness or attitude . . . [to] acknowledge the existence and validity of other ways of being, seeing, doing and communicating."[3]

Oral historians working with people with immigrant backgrounds need to be aware that cultural differences may have implications for an oral history project. In such a situation an oral historian needs the ability to communicate multiculturally to build rapport. Effective communication involves the ability to look beyond different behaviors and communication styles to determine the narrator's intention and meaning. Cultural differences may continue with immigrant communities even though the people within the community have moved from their country of origin. "For example, Tamilians have a distinct cultural identity, yet they can live in Sri Lanka, in the Indian state of Tamil Nadu, in the UK, in the US or anywhere else in the world."[4] The same could apply to any group of immigrants living in a different country.

How Common Are Cultural Differences? Statistics

Population statistics are not themselves an indicator of cultural attributes, either of individuals or of the population as a whole, but they underpin the composition and structure of a country's society.

In New South Wales (NSW), for example, Australia's most populated state, citizens come from 225 different birthplaces and have 245 different ancestries. People living in NSW speak over 215 languages and practice 125 different religions including Islam, Hinduism, Sikhism, Catholicism, and Christianity as well as many belief systems including atheism and Zoroastrianism. Arguably, the state of NSW is one of the most culturally and linguistically diverse communities in the world. NSW's multicultural society is wide-ranging and varied and a fundamental part of the state's identity.[5] NSW residents live in an eclectic mix of different linguistic, religious, racial, and ethnic backgrounds; NSW's multicultural society is in reality a community of communities. Australia is a country in which many people have made their home, with census statistics showing that forty-seven percent of the population was either born overseas or has a parent that was born overseas. Throughout Australia, similar to NSW, the Australian community is made up of people who have diverse backgrounds. Multiculturalism is a key aspect of Australian life. The cultural diversity of communities within Australia is actively supported and maintained. All Australians have the right to practice and maintain their cultural heritage, traditions, and language.[6]

The population of the United States, for example, is also racially and ethnically diverse. The United States 2010 census identifies six ethnic and racial categories amongst American people: White American, Native American, Alaska Native, Asian American, African American, and Native Hawaiian and

Other Pacific Islander. Some Other Race is a category used in the census to recognize people who identify themselves as having two or more racial backgrounds. The United States Census Bureau also classifies Americans as Hispanic or Latino and Not Hispanic or Latino. This recognizes Hispanic and Latino Americans as a genealogically diverse ethnicity that makes up the largest minority group in the United States.[7] The 2010 Census identified that in the United States, 12.9 percent of the population was born overseas.[8] The United States as a whole has a population which can trace back to many different cultures. Millions of Americans can trace back their origins to a different culture and may identify themselves as Chinese-American, Romanian-American, or Italian-American, and so on, even though the initial family immigration occurred generations previously.

The Concept of Citizenship

The perception of an individual's citizenship or nationality is changing. "With increasing globalisation, national borders are becoming blurred, and the notion of an individual having only one homeland is fast becoming outdated."[9] Worldwide, citizenship is frequently not limited to the formal citizenship of one particular country. Overall, society is becoming more homogenized because technology has changed the way we can communicate with each other and due to the relative ease of moving from one part of the world to another. People are more aware of variances throughout the world. Modern technologies give people virtual images and experiences of the world and the way people live in different countries. As well, real-life interaction between people of different cultures and all walks of life is widespread. Yet while cultural affinities and differences may be influenced by our modern world, overall, cultural traditions remain intact.[10]

Oral History Implications

Chances are, based on population demographic statistics, oral historians living in America or Australia or similarly culturally diverse countries may have opportunities to interview people with cultural backgrounds that differ from their own cultural backgrounds. Cultural differences should be taken into account. An oral historian has to determine the appropriate cultural protocols for proceeding with the oral history project—the correct ways to behave, communicate, consult, and show respect. For example, as an Australian raised in a home with Anglo-Celtic customs, I am at ease with asking people polite questions and with making polite requests for my needs, but my approach is not universally acceptable behavior. Another culture may consider directness impolite. If, during the interview, the oral historian's question is hard for the narrator to understand, a narrator may find it culturally inappropriate to ask for clarification because that implies criticism that the interviewer hasn't explained well. If the narrator wants to clarify what has been said, it may be difficult to interrupt the interview because the narrator may believe that interrupting a conversation is rude. Oral historians cannot presume their own ways of behaving and proceeding in an interview are "the right way" and relevant and appropriate to the needs and preferences of the narrator. People from different cultures may have different preferences and definitions of fitting behavior, which requires collaboration. Ignoring specific cultural differences that may impact on the authenticity of the interview is not practical. When interviewing people with cultural differences, the interviewer has to respond appropriately to difference and be guided by the narrator. There will also be cultural similarities. People everywhere have comparable fundamental needs and desires. An interview with a narrator who has a strong cultural affinity will not necessarily be problematic. Overall, the aim of the individual interview or project is to record unique narrative; therefore, being able to seamlessly accommodate a narrator's cultural background is crucial.

Communicating across cultures involves more than understanding across different groups of people; an oral historian should recognise the cultural nuances of the individual narrator. Effective cross-cultural interviewing involves the ability to set aside assumptions and focus on the needs and circumstances of the individual narrator. Intercultural interviewing should account for narrators' individual diversity, personality, values, and attitudes towards their culture—not just national cultural identity. Misunderstanding cultural differences may cause miscommunication in an interview and negatively affect interview rapport. Not accounting for difference may cause confusion, frustration, or even offence. Misunderstandings might happen when it comes to the interpretation of cultural differences; researching and learning about the meaning of cultural differences before an interview will help avoid misperception. Insight into the narrator's culture and customs is essential and will result in a better interview. Thorough research is also useful in alerting the oral historian to reconsider cultural stereotyping, biases, preconceptions, or generalisations. Not all Australians are tanned beach surfers, laconic, easygoing, and relaxed. Australians do not all greet each other with "g'day mate"!

Cultural Awareness Dimensions

Storti identifies four fundamental dimensions of culture that correspond to four broad categories of human experience. The values and beliefs associated with the four dimensions help explain why people of various cultural backgrounds behave in particular ways. The four dimensions are:

1. Concept of self – individualist and collectivist
2. Personal versus societal responsibility – universalist and particularist
3. Concept of time – monochromic and polychromic
4. Locus of control – internal and external[11]

Very briefly, (1) Concept of self – individualist and collectivist is about the way people in a culture identify primarily with themselves (individualist) or with the needs of a group, for example, family (collectivist). (2) Personal versus societal responsibility – universalist and particularist refers to how people balance personal responsibilities to people close to them and their responsibilities to society in general. Universalist and particularist responsibility is about how a society applies rules of morals and ethics. In universalism there is the understanding that what is right can be discovered, defined, and applied to every situation. Particularism is based on logic of the heart and human friendship. (3) Concept of time – monochromic and polychromic refers to how culture affects a person's concept of time and how people handle time. People perceive priorities and manage time in vastly different ways. In monochromic cultures activities are structured and scheduled. In polychromic cultures time is more fluid and less structured, and interruptions are readily accommodated. People from cultures which are monochromic value punctuality, and they may become frustrated by people who don't see punctuality as having a high priority. (4) Locus of control – internal and external refers to how a person's cultural background affects how much control it is believed a person has over life. Internal locus of control cultures believe what happens to a person is the person's doing and responsibility; people control the outcomes of their own lives. External locus of control cultures believe what happens to an individual is more out of the individual's own control and people tend to be more fatalistic about life. They are more likely to believe that the events in their lives are controlled by external factors such as luck, fate, and the behavior of other people. For all four dimensions, individual experiences vary and change depending on the context of a situation and can vary over time. The four dimensions are not strictly delineated. People do not fit rigidly within the dimensions; they tend towards a value system.

Accommodating Cultural Difference: Example of Accommodating Cultural Difference

Interviewing people for one oral history project required acceptance, acknowledgement, and adapting to some cultural behaviors that differed from what I am familiar with because of my Australian middle-class cultural sensibilities. Overall, changing my approach to conducting interviews was relatively easy.

Before the first interview of the project, I phoned to confirm the interview arrangements and heard a baby crying in the background. I asked (nicely) if the baby would be present during the interview. The interview was to be conducted in a small apartment. I explained politely that we needed, if possible, a quiet recording space. I was told that there was no noise; it was just a baby crying. The actual interview proceeded smoothly; the baby didn't cry and stayed in another room. However, after about an hour, which was fortunately towards the end of the interview, the mother of the baby, who was related to my narrator, interrupted the interview by standing in front of us with her baby. The mother was dressed, ready to go shopping, and the baby was in a stroller. My narrator was also part of the planned shopping trip and the bus they all had to catch was coming soon, so I had to pack up quickly and leave. No one had told me the interview session would be limited to a specific time, nor about the planned shopping trip. With my narrator I had developed a good rapport so there was no awkwardness; we were simply rushed at the end of the interview and did not have time for the usual winding down that typically occurs. While I was surprised by the sudden and unplanned conclusion to the interview, I did know about the difficulties my narrator and her family encountered living in a different country and adapting to a new culture and how they helped each other cope with the changes. This encounter clarified for me the importance of family responsibilities over something an individual member of the community was doing. This was the case even though the particular oral history project was conducted to record narrative for the benefit of the whole community. In this particular instance the people I was involved with demonstrated a collectivist concept of self and identified primarily with the needs of family. The people I was involved with in this instance demonstrated a polychromic approach to time priorities and management. In polychromic cultures time is more fluid and less structured, and interruptions are readily accommodated. My cultural standpoint with my organised interview time structure and schedule that also involved forward planning was monochromic.

A polychromic approach to time was demonstrated with another interview. I arrived at my narrator's home for the scheduled interview just in time to find him reversing his car out of his driveway. He had to give some family members a lift but was planning to return for the interview. Fortunately I saw him and the interview was confirmed for a slightly later time. If I had not fortuitously seen him, I simply would have phoned to verify what was happening. Within the community's cultural context, absolutely no rudeness was intended by my narrator, and adapting to a slightly different schedule was easily done. If a narrator with my own cultural background had done the same thing, I would have been bemused by the seeming inconsideration. This incident also demonstrated the custom of helping family and friends as a priority.

Another scheduled interview was more problematic. A local multicultural representative arranged that after my recording of an interview, a photographer and journalist from a large local newspaper would meet the narrator. They were engaged to take photographs and do a story based on a journalistic interview. A recording space was booked in the local library, and a local state government manager was also in attendance. Unfortunately the narrator did not come for the interview despite confirmation of all the arrangements and couldn't be contacted. Apart from a booked community venue, we had in attendance the interviewer and three other professionals—all busy monochromic time adherents! Everyone realised something must have happened. The intended narrator was not discourteous or inconsiderate. At the time of the interview family members arrived from overseas, so of course they were met. With family concerns as a justified priority, the proposed interview was not considered. Later on, the absent narrator was very apologetic; an opportunity to let us know she would not be at the interview had not been possible. Another person who lived nearby graciously agreed to be interviewed by an oral historian and a journalist and had her photograph taken with no notice at all; she was very accommodating and flexible and graciously welcomed us all into her home despite no prior warning.

When interviewing Savan, a Cambodian, I became aware that she placed me in a position of control because I was the interviewer. It seemed that for Savan the interview was hierarchical rather than collaborative even though my consistent awareness as an oral historian was for *shared authority*. When asked during the interview if she had anything more she wanted to talk about, Savan always deferred to me to follow up on what I wanted to know. In this respect Savan's locus of control was external. This was also indicated numerous times during the interview when she referred to how luck had been a determining fact in her life.

More Considerations: Gestures and Appropriate Communication Methods

Gestures, facial expressions, and body language are powerful means of communication, but they are not always consistent across cultures. Different cultures use gestures, facial expressions, and body language in different ways. The ways in which people greet each other, offer farewells, summon, indicate, show friendship and affection, insult, touch, and so on varies from culture to culture. Within an oral history context, an awareness of body language might be important. Hand gestures typically used during an oral history recording may represent a different meaning to narrators depending on their cultural background. For example, sometimes oral historians indicate a break is needed in an interview by raising their hand with the palm of the hand facing the narrator. Use of this signal with a Singaporean or Malaysian narrator might be confusing because the gesture in their cultures means trying to get someone's attention, such as when trying to get the attention of a waiter.[12]

The "ok" hand signal of circled thumb and index finger, sometimes used by an oral historian to start an interview after the final sound check is completed and the interview is ready to be recorded, can be interpreted very differently depending upon a narrator's cultural background. "The OK sign is terribly rude, even insulting, in diverse places like Russia, Germany and Brazil . . . in places like France and Japan it has entirely different meanings."[13] In some cultures direct eye contact is considered unseemly, intimidating, or rude. Avoidance of eye contact may be a mark of respect or polite behavior as opposed to an indicator of discourtesy or suspiciousness as in Anglo-Celtic culture.[14]

Another consideration is the most appropriate way to communicate with narrators that is culturally sensitive; face-to-face or by phone or e-mail. This is in addition to planning for the most appropriate way to communicate with narrators who find written English or speaking by telephone in English difficult.

An oral historian who is flexible towards cultural differences, takes the time to research potential different ways of behaving, and aims to build rapport with the narrator will go a long way to ensuring that an interview conducted with someone from a different culture proceeds smoothly and is rewarding. An oral historian needs to be aware that people can see the world and behave in different ways; difference should be respected.

Chapter 5

THE IMPORTANCE OF LANGUAGE

"Speak frankly"

—Interviewer

Use Plain, Clear, and Easily Understood English in Interviews

In many oral history interviews, "speak frankly" is a common suggestion given to a narrator in the preliminary recorded stages of an interview, before the actual interview begins. A narrator who is a native speaker of English or who speaks English with near-native proficiency will understand what the interviewer means. Anyone familiar with this English collocation will understand with no confusion whatsoever that the interviewer is asking the narrator to speak truthfully, honestly, and openly—a perfectly reasonable request. For someone who speaks English as a second language, the collocation might be confusing and could be taken literally; they might easily wonder, "Who's Frank?" The collocation's specific meaning may be completely lost on someone lacking excellent English-speaking proficiency and knowledge of the subtleties of the English language. The interview will begin in a confusing manner because the interviewer makes a request that lacks clarity and transparency. There are cultural implications as well; speaking frankly may be a culturally inappropriate request for some narrators because speaking frankly is inappropriate and rude.

If an oral history interviewer isn't careful, what is said in an interview may go straight over the narrator's head, they might not get the picture, they may not be able to make heads or tails of it, may not be able to figure it out, or it may be all Greek to them! Idiomatic language is especially perplexing, and use of idioms in English is commonplace. Idioms are mostly untranslatable,

Practicing Oral History with Immigrant Narrators by Carol McKirdy, pp. 75–83.

another frustration for second language speakers. It's almost impossible for native speakers to avoid speaking English without using the features that make it an expressive and vibrant language, but be aware that linguistic features and variations may need to be used with awareness and discretion. In the interview try to speak plainly so that the narrator understands exactly what is being talked about. Oral history, with its focus on listening and collaborative creation between the narrator and the interviewer, should not be hindered or disrupted by inattentiveness to the narrator's language competence. Awareness of the challenges of using a second language in an interview is not a hindrance. The challenges of interviewing a non-native English narrator enhance the interviewer's skills in working with a narrator to tell the story.

To be effective, an interviewer needs background knowledge of the subtleties and nuances of the narrator's first language. Language can express thoughts and concepts reflective of the narrator's culture, and the way thoughts and concepts are expressed varies depending on the language. There are words and expressions in English that do not have easily used equivalent understandings in other languages and vice versa. The narrator's first language might also affect the manner in which they respond in an interview. For example, in some languages usage indicates social hierarchy or appropriate responses for men and women or elders.

For speakers of English as a second language, interviewers should take into account the vagaries and intricacies of the English language. English, like most languages, is complex for users and more so when English is not the first language. Because English, in many respects, can be understood both literally and figuratively, it can be very perplexing. English is also an inventive and constantly evolving language, so words are added or change meaning frequently. In current Australian adolescent lingo the words "sick" and "filth(y)" mean wonderful! For some immigrant narrators, unnecessarily using figurative or difficult language in an interview adds extra demands to effective participation. The English language abounds in examples of abstract usage. Apart from collocations, linguistic features such as idioms, phrasal verbs, and euphemisms should be thought about carefully before being used in questions and responses in interview dialogue. Slang, colloquialisms, clichés, lingo, and metaphors should also be used with discretion because they might be totally perplexing to the narrator. Abbreviations are also hard for non-proficient English speakers to understand, especially when spoken. Double negatives should never be used as they are almost impossible to decipher. People who speak excellent English won't have as much trouble, but relatively new English speakers find the nuances of

English hard to grasp and fully understand. People who have been living in an English-speaking country for a long time may easily have difficulty. In a class conversation, a narrator who was a former high school teacher and an Australian resident and English speaker for over forty years was interviewed by a journalist about community volunteer work. The journalist used a phrasal verb to ask a question: "What do you get out of it?" In class, the narrator had to ask what the question meant.

Examples of Difficult Language

Collocations

A collocation is a familiar grouping of words that are often used together and so convey meaning by association, for example: "War torn," "in as much," "set in stone," "heavy fighting," "to date," "strong denial," and "in so much."

An interviewer might be tempted to ask a narrator who has experienced war a question about living in a "war torn" country. The question rephrased and without the collocation would be easier to understand.

Idioms

Idioms are mostly phrases that have a literal meaning in one context but a totally different sense in another. Idioms say one thing but mean another. They also don't usually follow normal grammatical patterns or rules. There are thousands of idioms in the English language. Even sophisticated speakers of English will be challenged by the meanings behind many of them. Avoid asking, for example:

"Was it raining cats and dogs before the flood?"
"When did you decide to turn over a new leaf?"
"Where was the whistle blower?"
"Did that rub salt into the wound?"
"Who was the black sheep of the family?"

Idioms are sometimes culturally specific, for example, "skyscrapers." Many cultures, however, may be aware of a "black sheep" in the family. Idioms in English frequently have counterparts in other languages with local context. Be careful if you have a launch event for your oral history project and ask everyone to "bring a plate!"

Phrasal Verbs

A phrasal verb combines verbs with an adverb or preposition that work in conjunction with each other to create meaning. The individual words can't be analyzed or translated individually; the phrasal verb has to be understood as a whole and the meaning is often unpredictable. The following are examples of phrasal verbs: "Stand by," "put up with," "looking forward to," "dress down," "takes after," and "sitting in for."

An interviewer might ask if a narrator is "looking forward to" retirement. "Looking forward to" is an example of a phrasal verb that is very recognizable, but nonetheless it may confuse some people.

Euphemisms

A euphemism is an inoffensive word or expression used instead of an unpleasant, rude, harsh, or blunt word or expression. Examples are "laid off," "blue-eyed boy," "passed away," "white lie," or "in the family way."

If a narrator is talking about losing a job, an interviewer might be tempted to ask the date they were laid off. It would be better to ask for the date they stopped working.

Double Negatives

A double negative in an English sentence occurs when two forms of negation are used. The negative words cancel each other out to create a positive understanding. An oral history interview question that has a double negative is hard to understand as well as being grammatically incorrect. Double negatives are acceptable in informal conversation and are sometimes used by songwriters, for example: "Ain't no mountain high enough," "I can't get no satisfaction," and "We don't need no education." They are inappropriate for oral history because the narrator finds it hard to determine what the question is asking. Double negative questions are confusing and illogical.

"Did you not escape without your family?"
"Was your village not unattractive?"
"Was there nothing less terrible than the fire?"
"When you look back don't you regret not becoming a nurse?"
"Do you mean you hadn't scarcely enough food?"

Grammar

Using English grammar correctly is invariably challenging for an English second language user. In the context of an oral history interview, incorrect English grammar can inadvertently alter the meaning of the narrative. Oral history interviewers should be aware of the relatively simple but potentially meaning-changing errors in English usage that might characterise an interview. Engage with the narrator by listening carefully and clarify inconsistencies. Some of the more common difficulties narrators from a second language background have in an interview setting are as follows.

Tense: Telling Time through the Verb Tense

Tense is very difficult for non-native speakers of English to master. Described simply, English tense tells when an action occurs, indicates how long the action takes, and whether it is completed. The most common tenses are:

Past – Simple past: something which has happened in the past and is finished. (I lived in Italy.)

Past continuous: tells us about something which continued in the past. (I was living in Italy.)

Past perfect: tells us about something which happened in the past before something else. (I had lived in Italy.)

Present – Simple present: tells about something which always happens or something which usually happens. (I live in Italy.)

Present continuous: tells us about something which is happening at the moment. (I am living in Italy.)

Present perfect: tells us about something which was completed before this moment. (I have lived in Italy.)

Future: tells us about something which will happen after this moment. (I will live in Italy.)

Future continuous: tells us about something which will continue in the future. (I will be living in Italy.)

Future perfect: tells us about something which will be completed at a future date. (I will have lived in Italy.)

A narrator who finds English tense difficult to grasp may be confused with the differences between the different ways of saying when something happened in the past, how something is happening now, and how something may happen in the future. The narrator may lack knowledge of how sentences are constructed. In an English sentence, the first verb establishes the tense of later verbs in the sentence. Listeners are confused if this pattern isn't followed. The narrator might not know how to link what is being said now with what happened in the past. As oral history is ultimately a record of the past, it's essential to establish with the narrator exactly when something occurred in the narrative. A narrator may very easily use the incorrect tense. The interviewer has to listen carefully to ensure the narrator doesn't inadvertently miscommunicate when something happened. Subtleties of timing may be explained inaccurately because of poor verb formation choice. By listening attentively the interviewer will realise clarification is needed.

Historical events are sometimes recorded in a tense known as the historic present. For events that happened in the past, historic present tense is used to make the historical event always seem to exist for the listener or reader in the present, as if the event is actually happening. The narrative creates the effect of immediacy. Narrators recounting their narratives this way have not confused tenses; rather they are indicating the vividness of the story they have to tell. For example, "It is 1976 in Saigon, Vietnam, and I am waiting in the dark with my uncle. We keep still and quiet. We don't want to be noticed. The boat pulls in to the shore and we board."

Syntax May Be Irregular

Syntax in English refers to the positioning of words in a sentence, written or spoken, and the arrangement of words and phrases to create well-formed, understandable, grammatically correct sentences. Syntax is how the various parts of speech such as nouns, verbs, adjectives, prepositions, and so on connect together. Syntax helps the facilitation of being understood with language rules. For native speakers of English, using correct syntax isn't difficult, comes naturally, and is generally acquired intuitively by the time school starts. Native speakers can differentiate syntactically correct from incorrect combinations of words, even though they may not be able to explain why. They may not know the grammatical rules. Second language users need to understand the word order of English to be understandable and communicate effectively in English. Correct syntax is difficult to master and narrators may revert to their intuitive understanding of their own native language structure and impose it, unproductively, on English grammar. For example, a Spanish narrator might say "is hot" rather than "it is hot." The subject of the sentence, in this case "it," is left out as in Spanish. In English, adjectives precede nouns, but in French, Spanish, and Arabic, describing words come after the noun; a French-speaking narrator might say, "We had a dog large and a rabbit small."

Vocabulary

The narrator's vocabulary may be limited, and they might use words that don't express what has happened to them as accurately, descriptively, and effectively as befitting the narrative being recorded. As well as not knowing apt words to use, words that are used may be used incorrectly. Rather than saying, "We went in different cars," the narrator may say, "We went in difference cars" because of a lack of skill in using correct word formation. In this example meaning is not affected and the narrative is perfectly understandable. If you suspect that your narrator has used an unsuitable word to suit the story, clarify the word meaning with them. Help your narrators with vocabulary; they'll appreciate your assistance in helping them tell their narratives as concisely as possible. Second language users sometimes need prompting about words that are actually in their vocabulary but have been momentarily forgotten. Being able to access bilingual dictionaries, hardcopy or device, during the interview may be a source of comfort to a narrator who may anticipate problems choosing the right words to say. Accessing either type of dictionary will be noisy and potentially affect the sound quality of the recording. To avoid sound issues, let the recorder run as the dictionary is consulted, resume the interview, then edit out the disruption to the interview later.

Prepositions

An incorrectly used preposition can sound odd and momentarily puzzle the listener. English preposition usage is notoriously difficult to master. Prepositions are usually used in front of a noun or pronoun, indicating the relationship with other words in the sentence. A preposition explains to a listener when and where something occurred as well as how it occurred. A narrator might say something like: "We went at (on) Saturday" or "I travelled under (through) the tunnel."

The Definite and Indefinite Article

The meanings of "the," "a," and "an" before nouns might be confused. "The factory" has a very different meaning from "a factory," for example.

Pronouns

In English, pronouns are used for various reasons, in place of nouns. For example, "he" is used when referring to a male, "she" refers to a female, and "it" refers to something inanimate, or an animal of unknown sex. In numerous languages pronoun usage is very different from English pronoun usage, and this can lead to misunderstanding. Speakers not used to using the pronouns "he" and "she" instead of names often swap between "he" and "she," further confusing listeners. In an interview you may have to clarify the sex of someone being spoken about, especially if you are unfamiliar with first names from your narrator's first language.

Unclear Pronunciation

The way a narrator speaks in English might be hard to understand and can greatly affect how the narrative is understood both by the interviewer during the interview process and by listeners later on. A "foreign" accent may be difficult to follow; there are many reasons why English is hard to pronounce clearly. Learning how to say some of the phonemes (sounds) of English is taxing; some English phonemes do not exist in other languages, so they are especially difficult for new users to pronounce. English speakers from Japan do not have the sounds /dg/ /f/ /i/ /th/ /oo/ /v/ and the schwa, and Spanish speakers don't have /dg/ /j/ /sh/ /th/ /z/. There are similar difficulties for other languages. English sounds that are mispronounced or not pronounced have the potential to alter the meaning of what is said, for example, not pronouncing word endings such as "s" or "es" to indicate plurals. Speakers might pronounce the start of some words but neglect to say the ending, the final consonant, vowel, or syllable, for example, ten/tent, fi/five, teach/teacher. Endings to indicate past tense sound strange if the narrator hasn't learned that the extra "ed" syllable is used when a verb ends in "t" or "d" as in shout/ed and land/ed. The narrator might easily say, bak/ed, caus/ed, or long/ed, and this can be confusing for listeners. Some errors that second language users make in their speech originate from first language expertise that doesn't transfer to English usage. As well, if English is spoken with varying degrees of incorrect rhythm, intonation, pitch, or stress, a narrator might sound angry, rude, impolite, uninterested, or unintelligible, even though that is not the intention. Speech delivery may be abrupt or staccato.

The interviewer should listen carefully as the narrator speaks. Paraphrase a response for the listeners' benefit or for clarification by the narrator. Ask the question again or rephrase the question. Ask questions that encourage and support narrators to tell their stories in shorter chunks of information with pauses between each new chunk of information. Telling the story in a single stream without a break makes it harder to understand. Also encourage the narrator to speak slowly.

Transcriptions of Imperfect English

Transcripts are verbatim versions of the spoken words of the narrator. A transcript matches the interview as closely as possible. If the narrator's English is consistently irregular, a transcript will be difficult to comprehend. A comprehensive summary or annotated log is usually a better option in this situation. Transcription vagaries are well known. Narrators don't speak in sentences that transfer seamlessly to correct written English sentences. Spoken and written English differs. When talking, speakers repeat themselves, mumble, stumble over words, leave out punctuation, forget to finish words and ideas, and lose the thread of what they are saying amongst other variations. Issues are compounded when the narrator does not have full control over the language used in the interview.

Attempts to "correct" the English, apart from dubiously changing the nature and intention of a transcription, are problematic. In an effort to create grammatically sensible English sentences, the meaning of the narration may be altered. Significantly, the transcription will not be the actual words as spoken by the narrator. With a summary or annotated log, there is scope to write the true intended meaning because both approaches require reflection on what the narrator said rather than writing the words verbatim. Logs and summaries also allow for cooperative reconsideration of the spoken narrative with the narrator. They also enable grammatical correctness.

Chapter 6

USING AN INTERPRETER IN
AN ORAL HISTORY INTERVIEW

"My English is terrible."

—Narrator

If inadequate English-speaking skills or a perceived lack of ability to speak English well enough prevents a narrator telling his or her story in English, use an interpreter. The narrator recounts in a language in which he or she feels confident and competent. Overcoming the English language communication barrier ensures the narrator can participate effectively in an interview. The interpreter becomes the key to unlocking the non-English spoken narrative. The interpreting method most appropriate for an oral history interview is known as consecutive interpreting.[1] In consecutive interpreting the interpreter speaks after the interviewer has spoken, then after the non-English-language narrator has responded, with pauses allowed for the interpreter to translate either into English or the narrator's language. The words of the interviewer and the narrator are spoken in full before the interpreter takes over.

Using an interpreter has to be something the narrator is comfortable with and agrees to do. The decision about whether to use an interpreter belongs to the narrator; it may prove overwhelming. Knowing how to work with an interpreter is important for everyone involved. A narrator may have concerns about using an interpreter or the interpreting process. If the narrator is hesitant, explain the role of an interpreter in an oral history interview and the benefits of using an interpreter, not just for the narrator but for the overall project. Explain the practicalities of using an interpreter—the arrangements for speaking, responding, and translating. Explain how doing the interview in the narrator's first language will be easier and give the opportunity to express exactly what the narrator wants to say.

Reluctance to Use an Interpreter

There can be many reasons for reluctance to use an interpreter. The narrator might be embarrassed about admitting to a lack of acquired English-speaking skills despite the fact that acquiring second language proficiency, especially in English, is known to be difficult. The embarrassment may be culturally based. Narrators who have experienced human rights violations may be hesitant to trust an outsider in the interview process. There may be fears that the interpreter will pass on pejorative comments to authorities. There may also be concern about confidentiality, so it's important to reassure the narrator that the interpreter must maintain confidentiality, be impartial, and abide by ethical practice and the guidelines established for the project, as well as abide by the stringent code of conduct for interpreters.

Assessing the Need for a Professional Interpreter

The need to use an interpreter will become obvious as soon as the potential narrator engages or attempts to engage in conversation. Or, the narrator may have requested the use of an interpreter. Or, someone involved with the oral history project may have recommended the use of an interpreter for a particular narrator. Common sense is needed to assess and confirm the potential of a narrator to participate constructively in an oral history interview in English as a second language. Typically, very low-level English proficiency speakers will recognise key English identification words (name, address, age, nationality, etc.) and survival words (police, hospital, stop, bathroom, etc.), and they will be familiar with greetings such as "hello" and "goodbye." As people become more proficient, they are able to converse with more fluency, sophistication, and detail. However, a narrator must be able to demonstrate English language competency beyond the standard, predictable, and probably much-used, rehearsed, and practised English speech associated with commonplace situations, daily life, and employment. Narrators who have acquired English language skills beyond basic proficiency will almost certainly make grammatical errors, use correct tense form inconsistently, have broken syntax, make errors with pronoun agreement, and struggle sometimes with using prepositions appropriately. Also, their pronunciation, although understandable, may be flawed, but they will know what you are asking them, and they will be able to answer accurately. The interviewer may need to clarify responses that are unclear because of the narrator's less-than-perfect control over the English language. Ultimately, the oral historian has to make a decision about the best way the narrator can participate in an interview—English or another language.

Language Assessment Tools

Assessable evidence to justify the need for an interpreter can be obtained by using language assessment tools such as the Australian Core Skills Framework (ACSF),[2] the Test of English as a Foreign Language (TOEFL),[3] or the International English Language Testing System for non-native English speakers (IELTS).[4] All assess and map aspects of oral language capability, ranking spoken English proficiency from non-user/beginner through to advanced/expert English-speaking skills. Using assessment tools like these or similar would be very useful for justifying funding applications that include quotes for interpretation services. The oral history project designers would be able to justify the additional costs of interpreter services with specific factual evidence such as the number of narrators at ACSF Oracy 1 and 2, for example.[5] The disadvantages of these and the many other similar instruments available in English-speaking countries are that, depending on the instrument, there is often a cost associated with taking a test or the assessment has to be carried out by a qualified assessor. However, the general descriptors of the assessment tools and levels are freely available online and could realistically serve as general indicators for an oral history project wanting some sort of empirical evidence to justify the need for, and cost of, interpreting services. As well, immigrant narrators may already have applicable assessment results that can be used as confirmation of suitability as a candidate for using an interpreter in an interview.

Arranging an Interpreter

Professional interpreter services work with qualified and experienced interpreters who are bound by their industry's code of conduct. Depending on the context of the interpreting services needed, the services try to match the interpreter to the context and subject matter of the interpreting task. A competent interpreter will be not only bilingual, but also biculturally aware. For an oral history interview, the interpreter, because of linguistic background, is likely to be relatively familiar with the cultural, social, religious, and political context of the narrator's home language, and this is helpful as it gives background knowledge for the interview. The interpreter should have a positive regard for the narrator's culture and language and be aware of significant cultural and linguistic influences that may impact on the interview. Before hiring an interpreter, establish the specific language or dialect spoken by the narrator to avoid ineffective or useless interpreting. India, for example, has several hundred languages,[6] and China has over fifty languages;[7] linguistically diverse Africa has languages numbering in the thousands.[8] Don't make assumptions. A Vietnamese person may speak a Chinese language rather than Vietnamese, for example. The interpreter should have native-level proficiency in the appropriate language/dialect and the ability to provide highly accurate interpretation.

The narrator may prefer and feel more comfortable using a male or a female interpreter. It is especially important to check if the narrator has a religious, ethnic, or political preference for the interpreter. A narrator who follows a particular religion, for example, might feel compromised using an interpreter who identifiably follows a different faith, especially if there is residual animosity because of past conflict in the home country and even more so if the interview will be exploring the narrator's history in relation to the conflict. This may not be an issue for the narrator, but it is best to check; sensitivity is required.

Avoid using family members or friends as interpreters. It may be difficult for them to be objective and impartial. They may have a conflict of interest or be narrators for the project, in which case their narration may be unduly influenced through their being used as an interpreter for other narrators. Personal relationships may influence the quality of the translation. Family and friend interpreters are not bound by the same code of conduct as a professional interpreter. Non-English-speaking immigrants typically rely on their English-speaking children to support them in everyday activities, but child interpreters are not appropriate for oral history interviews. Family/friend proficiency in the chosen language cannot be guaranteed. A similar situation applies to interpreters who come from closely linked community groups.

Working with an Interpreter

If an interpreter is required, securing the interpreter's services becomes part of the pre-organization for the interview; coordinating convenient times for all concerned is understandably more difficult. The additional cost associated with using an interpreter has to be factored in.

Working with an interpreter is challenging. Interpreting itself is a taxing profession, consecutive interpreters have to translate "in situ," and the job requires intense concentration and attention to detail. With good preparation, an oral historian can make the interpreter's job easier and more effective and achieve the best possible outcome for an interpreted interview.

As well as helping the interpreter beforehand, the oral historian has to help the narrator understand how the interview will proceed with an interpreter. Either ask the interpreter to explain the process or ask a trusted person who speaks the same language as the narrator. Introduce the narrator and interpreter to each other before the formal interview begins, but try to engage with the narrator before the interpreter arrives to validate the narrator-interviewer relationship. The interpreter in reality becomes a very important part of the oral history process, but the primary relationship is between the oral historian and the narrator. This should be obvious to the narrator.

- Develop a collaborative, trusting, respectful relationship with the interpreter.
- Make time to brief the interpreter before the interview so that you can familiarise the interpreter with your oral history project and anything regarding the project that you think will help the interpreter's understanding when interpreting the narrative.
- Ensure the interpreter is informed about your recording procedures and equipment. Ask the interpreter to follow standard protocols, such as turning off mobile phones, and to avoid moving in and out of microphone range.
- Establish procedures for the interpreting session such as break times and hand signals typically used in an oral history interview, like hand raising to pause the recording.
- Make sure the interpreter knows about vocabulary and terms, especially jargon and slang, specific to the project.
- Pay particular attention to potential causes of concern or distress that might come up in the interview so that the interpreter is forewarned. For example, you may plan to ask your narrator about experiences during civil unrest or diaspora and the response may be traumatic for the narrator to speak about and for the interpreter and oral historian to listen to. If necessary, be prepared to assist the interpreter with emotional support because of the narrative given in the interview. Also be aware that some interpreters may have experienced similar distressing situations to those experienced by the narrator and may therefore need support.

- Arrange seating so both the interviewer and the interpreter can maintain eye contact with the narrator.
- Arrange seating so that all voices are picked up by the microphone(s).
- Give the interpreter a copy of your planned interview questions and/or prompts before the interview so that the interpreter can become familiar with them, clarify points if needed, and in turn, clarify the structure, content, and contextual framework of your interview. Also tell the interpreter that you will probably diverge from your planned interview format depending on the responses of the narrator and the dialogue that emerges from the interview. The aim is to give background knowledge to help the interpreter become as familiar as possible with the interview before interpreting begins.
- Engage with your narrator the same way you would in a standard interview when interviewing via an interpreter.
- Be aware that some narrators may sometimes understand and respond directly to an interview question in English without waiting for the translation.
- Speak to the narrator directly and not to the interpreter. You won't understand what is being said until each part of the translation is done, but nonetheless focus on the narrator, show interest, and maintain eye contact as you would normally. As with any oral history interview, you need to build trust and rapport. The interpreter is a means to an end; the interview relationship, as usual, is between the narrator and the interviewer. As the oral historian you should be just as aware of the narrator's body language and the tone of what is being said even though the language being spoken is foreign to you. The interpreter's role is to translate what is said; the interpreter does not offer personal comments or opinions. Nor should interpreters make comments such as "the narrator is sad/angry/upset/anxious"—their task is to interpret the narrator's words as accurately as possible with integrity.
- Structure your sentences and questions and responses carefully.
- Don't speak at length and speak clearly, without haste.
- Allow time for the interpreter to relay what you have asked and for the narrator's response to be translated. Good oral history questioning and interview technique in which one question at a time is asked and double negatives are not used is undoubtedly more important when using an interpreter.
- Make your speech as plain as possible; avoid idiomatic expressions and phrasal verbs that may not translate accurately. "When did you break

down?" has two meanings if the phrasal verb is understood, let alone what it means when translated! If the narrator is talking about having left home to fly to America and you ask them how it felt to "hit the road," does the English idiom translate with a similar meaning into the narrator's language? Will the narrator understand that you are asking how it felt to leave home, or might the narrator wonder why you are asking about land travel when it has been made clear that the narrator travelled by plane? There is not always a direct translation from English into another language and vice versa, so you need to work closely with the interpreter to achieve an honest and accurate translation.

- Plan your interview session timing carefully. Interviewing through an interpreter takes about twice as long, so the narrator is more likely to tire. A longer interview session has implications for battery-operated recording equipment—will battery life last for the interview duration?
- Adjust the standardised introduction at the start of the interview to include the interpreter's name and details.
- Debrief the interpreter to discuss any issues or concerns that arose during the interview.
- If subsequent recording sessions are required, do your utmost to secure the services of the same interpreter for continuity and transparency for the narrator.

Transcription

Transcribing an interpreted oral history interview adds challenges to the well-known difficulties and vagaries of transcription. Transcription adds an extra layer of difficulty; the translator-transcriber has an onerous job because the narrator's words have already been processed from one language to another. Added to this situation is that the transcription process is twofold—a transcription from spoken English to written English and a transcription from the spoken second language to the written spoken language so that the narrator is able to confirm and clarify the interview content in the narrator's language of choice.

Using Bilingual Interviewers

Bilingual oral history interviewers with native proficiency in both English and the language of the narrator are a wonderful asset to an immigrant oral history project for all the obvious reasons. The subtleties and nuances of each language are understood by the narrator during the interview and the interviewer is able to pick up on these for the benefit of the project. During the interview, the interviewer and narrator can, if appropriate, speak in either language to enable the best possible record of the narrator's story. Logistical matters such as coordinating meeting times are more easily arranged when arrangements are made in a language easily understood by the narrator. Pre-interviews and post-interviews don't have to be conducted in person; telephone communication is a possibility.

The use of an interpreter may be the only way of ensuring an oral history project is inclusive, so that all voices can be heard and recorded.

Chapter 7

Using Images to Support Oral History Narrative

"She showed me . . . a very tiny picture of her husband. . . .
the photographer enlarged it . . . a picture of her husband
who had died, it was the only one she had. . . . she opened
it up . . . her husband life sized . . . she kissed it and kissed it
and kissed it and cried. . . . I realise now that not only do they
leave their everything they have very few precious things to
bring and they don't have many photos, some do, but some
have no photos . . . and we take photos for granted."[1]

The adage "a picture is worth a thousand words," or its several forms, is familiar to oral historians who recognise the capacity of an image to trigger recall, enhance the detail and scope of the overall oral history project, and add subjective, visual elements that complement the personal history that is recorded. Photographs supplement the narrative because of their special significance as very precious or significant possessions from the past as well as their connections to a different, past life.

Using Photographs in Immigrant Narratives

Photographs give an apparent narrative, but if the details and stories about the photographs are discussed in an oral history interview setting, photographs have the potential to provide further, richer narrative. They can play

Practicing Oral History with Immigrant Narrators by Carol McKirdy, pp. 93–107.

Figure 7.1: With the only photo she has of her late husband, Sutherland, NSW, 2006.
Photo courtesy ©Keith Saunders.

a more substantial role than documents used to add visual interest to an oral history project. There are also potential narrator stories about photographs that are missing. There may be photos that have been lost or misplaced or not taken on the journey to a new life in a different country; all are situations an immigrant narrator may be familiar with. The narrator may grieve for the photographs that were lost or that would have been taken if circumstances had been better.

The Importance of Images to Narrators, Some Examples

Anwar was born in Basra, a large city in Iraq, in 1962. In 1980, when she was in Year 11 (11th Grade/Junior) at high school, the Iran-Iraq War began. Anwar spoke about how ordinary people tried to live a normal life. During the war Anwar finished school and went to university. She married, but there weren't many people at her wedding because Basra had become a dangerous place in which to live. Anwar's family had stayed behind in the city because they wanted to be close to the eldest son, who was in the Iraqi army. In her interview Anwar deeply regretted the loss of her wedding video. She had to leave it behind when she was eventually forced to move to Baghdad.[2]

A photograph of his wife as a young woman, stained by seawater, is one of the most treasured possessions owned by narrator X. His oral history is published under a pseudonym because of enduring enmity from his home country. Male escapees like him, who leave a country because of persecution, in search of freedom and the chance of a better and safe life, are nervous about repercussions years later. Narrator X escaped by boat and used to stare at the photo of his wife because he loved and missed her and to help him maintain his spirits and resolve to start a new life in a different country despite the terrible odds against his survival. He sailed into open sea in an unseaworthy boat, normally used in coastal waters. His wife planned her escape separately to give better chances of survival for the family as a whole and for the safety of their children, who were divided between the parents. All survived. In Australia the entire family is successful. The parents, both well beyond retirement age, contribute to Australian society through volunteer work with people less fortunate. The children are all specialists in their fields of expertise.

For immigrant narrators a lack of photos can tell a great deal about their past history and the importance of having photos. Savan Hin came to Australia with no photographs apart from one large group photo that was taken when she lived in a Thai refugee camp. Her face shows as a small, blurry dot. She was forced to leave her home by Pol Pot enforcers with no warning and had to leave all her possessions behind, including photographs. Later, when she was safely living in Australia, Savan wrote to family members who had survived Pol Pot's tyrannical rule and asked them to send her family photographs. The photos she received make up a small but important collection for Savan and her family. Savan's digital savvy and expertise with handling images, their storage, where to source associated images online, and the significance and application of images on social media platforms is highly skilful and sophisticated. Replacing and owning significant photographs from the past and access to other similar images is very important to her. She's very familiar with websites that have images relevant to her background.[3]

The thumb-sized photo referred to in the quote at the start of this chapter was carried during a long, dangerous journey by foot and at night, through

Figure 7.2: Seawater stained photo, Vietnam circa 1977. Photo courtesy: name withheld.

Sudan to Kenya and then to Australia by plane. Gaye's eventual gift of a husband and father's photo, lifelike, was a momentous family event.

Gaye also recounted the story of a young Sudanese mother whose baby died in her arms as she was running to escape enemy militia during hostilities in Sudan. The mother placed her baby's body under a bush. There was no time to bury the baby because of the dangerous circumstances. It is hard to comprehend the horror and sadness of this situation. Gaye spoke of listening to the mother's heartbreaking story in order to give support, and she spoke, as well, of the additional sadness of the mother because she did not have any photographs of her baby, only memories. Gaye requested a second interview be conducted because in her first interview we had not talked about the importance of photographs to the Sudanese refugees she befriended and helped through her volunteer church work and personally. She wanted to redress not talking about the importance of photographs to refugees who had experienced great loss.[4]

Practical Methods for Using Photographs with Immigrant Narrators

For immigrant narrators who find communication in English challenging, photographs are especially useful because an image offers the narrator a reference point for discussion. The prompting offered by a photograph is very helpful. Narrators don't have to struggle as much with finding correct vocabulary because images remind them of the words they need and limit somewhat what they have to say in English as the narrative is focussed. Telling their whole story in language they find challenging can be overwhelming. For narrators with a relatively limited English vocabulary there will not be as many words to say and there will be less internal translating from the first language to English. As well, they can confirm language and terminology with the interviewer before recording. Conducting an oral history interview that uses photographs is different from a traditionally conducted interview. The process offers the opportunity to take breaks and a chance for narrators to check, confirm, and discuss what they will say about the photographs. The less structured approach also means that a narrator has time to consult a bilingual translation dictionary. In a traditionally conducted interview photographs can, in fact, be a nuisance because of the noise they make when handled and their possible disruption to a free-flowing interview. If parts of the interview are planned to be used as sound installations, the noise photographs make can render the audio recording useless for that particular purpose. As well, once the interview starts a narrator can't consult a dictionary unless a deliberate break is made during the recording. Digital translation dictionaries, especially dictionaries on smartphones, can't be as easily referred to, if wanted, because of the time they take to turn on after being turned off for the interview, following normal interview protocol.

Short Interviews Using Photographs to Tell Immigrant History

Short interviews are brief interviews, about five minutes in length, based on selected photographs chosen by the narrator as being of particular importance and significance. Five minutes is an approximate guide; there are no "rules" regarding length. Recording discrete, relatively short narratives in response to individual photographs is a possible variation of the usually much longer traditional oral history interview. A short recording is especially suitable for immigrant narrators who have limited capacity to engage at length in English. The narrator needs access to photographs capable of eliciting a response for personal history, so the technique is not always applicable. People with immigrant backgrounds don't necessarily have photos to talk about. If photographs are available and the narrator is willing to give a personal narrative in response to a selection of photographs that have personal historical significance, the approach works well as a different way of recording narrative. The narrative will probably not be as comprehensive or free-flowing as an oral narrative recorded in the traditional manner, but it will allow the narrator to tell the story or, at least, relevant aspects. This method of recording oral history allows for the collection of more specific information because the recording is in response to particular images. Narrators could be interviewed in response to personal photographs or personally applicable photographs sourced from the *public domain*, or talk about photographs taken of personally and culturally relevant objects to preserve provenance, for example. As always, the focus is on the narrator's unique circumstances and story, so other short interview scenarios could evolve and be appropriate. Creating audio recordings that are brief and discrete and linked to images is an appropriate alternative means of gathering history for any oral history project. It is a good method for recording stories from elders who may possibly tire in a longer interview.

Using Sourced Photographs

If photographs of personal significance are not available, it may be possible to use other photos sourced from friends, community, or similar organizations, or from the vast array of *copyright*-free images available online. The photographs used in short interviews don't necessarily have to include significant people, such as family, friends, and associates. Photographs can be of homes; locations; land usage; plants; cars, trains, bicycles, motorcycles, rickshaws, tuk-tuks, sea craft, and other means of transport; native animals of the home country; political leaders; the military; maps and flags; home resources; or food—in fact, anything with links to the narrator's past. A well-chosen photograph, though not unique to the narrator, will have a familiarity that enables the narrator to speak about the past using the picture as a catalyst. A Hungarian narrator looked at images, taken during the Hungarian Uprising,[5] that were uploaded to the Internet. She told me that the images were just as she remembered when she walked from her workplace with colleagues to see what was happening in Budapest firsthand in late October, 1956.

Narrating about Artefacts and Memorabilia Belonging to the Narrator

If a narrator has objects or artefacts of significance to the narrator as an individual or for their community, from the past or currently used, these can be photographed and talked about for the oral history project. The narrator then talks about the photographed items in the short interview. This helps create narratives as well as assist in defining provenance of the items. Narrators may have letters, war postcards, immigration documentation, and diaries, for example. A narrator might want to talk about household items, food, cooking implements, ornaments, clothing, family jewellery, and so on. The range of items that could be photographed is limited only by what the narrator has available and wants to talk about in an interview. If the overall oral history project is focussing on a theme such as traditional dress or performance, for example, then limitations are obviously imposed. The shorter recordings create a historical record for the objects of importance to the narrator. The interviewer should structure the interview so as to elicit specific historical information such as dates, origin, ownership, background, derivation, source, and attribution as well as stories about the objects. The stories and history behind the artefacts, collected in a short interview format, preserve history as a legacy for future generations. For example, a narrator might provide particular details about an item of clothing: the who, what, when, where, why, and how of the garment. Later generations will know why an elder in their family wore that particular item. If provenance isn't secured, the whys and wherefores are forgotten. The stories that objects tell will depend on the contexts in which they are situated, as well as the backgrounds and connections of their owners. Photographed objects can tell and reveal a variety of stories in short interviews.

How to Structure and Conduct a Short Interview

- Follow all established oral history collection protocols and methodology including gaining permission to use the narrator's personal images as well as words. Take particular care with copyright if using stock images.
- If the recording is focussing on images of objects and artefacts, organise for photographs to be taken before recording commences.
- For images, establish and integrate a classification system that links the interview recording to the photograph. This can be as simple as the interviewer briefly describing the image before the narration at the start of each short recorded interview. A more systematic approach would be for the interviewer to establish a classification system such as Photograph 1/Audio Recording 1 as well as a brief description.
- If an object or picture is presented within the interview unexpectedly, describe it yourself. For example, a narrator may present a book with an illustration or image. Say words such as "Narrator is showing his passport picture/Narrator is showing her grandmother's bracelet."
- Get as much detail as possible about presented objects that have been photographed.
- Include a comprehensive summary and timed log for each interview that clearly links the photographs and objects to the narrator's words. Follow the method you established in the recording.

Publishing Short Interviews

Short interviews can be published in much the same way as standard oral histories. An advantage of the smaller digital files created is that they can be more easily uploaded to, for example, e-mails, social media sites, web 2.0 technologies such as wikis and blogs, and in digital publishing. As well consider these options:

- In a digitally created photobook with the text or text summary, possibly in both English and the first language of the narrator, alongside the image. Some photobooks allow the creator to upload audio and video files as well as images and text.
- As brief digital sound files packaged with copies of the images or video. This can be achieved using *digital storytelling* techniques or programs such as PowerPoint, Prezi, or Apple's Keynote.
- On a purpose-designed site such as U.S.-based Legacy Stories,[6] which has a system for collecting legacy photo narrations called Pict-Oral

Memoirs. Legacy Stories also has free apps for iPhone, iPad, and Android smart phones for recording memories linked to pertinent legacy photos that enable heritage to be kept for future generations (Pict-Oral Memories™). Legacy Stories contends that reminiscing with old photos and recording one-off recollections is the easiest and most enjoyable way to document and pass down legacy stories.

In about an hour, about three short recordings of roughly five minutes duration could be created, depending on the stamina of the narrator. The length of short interviews will depend on each narration session; the suggestion for five minutes is simply a guide which endorses brevity rather than length.

Advantages of Short Interviews

An advantage of the method is that narrators, who may find participating in a traditional interview tiring, find working in short segments less onerous. Narrators who think that they don't have sufficient recall detail or have "nothing to say" find the intrinsic prompting offered by an image useful because the focus is taken away from "remembering" to speaking about the content of a picture. The interviewer tries to establish what is obvious as well as the less obvious stories that lie behind the photo. The interview can easily be conducted in short sessions with breaks in between.

Speaking specifically in response to photographs preserves the integrity of personal images. Probably most people are familiar with family images of people, places, and things that nobody remembers; once-familiar and significant faces become strangers with names and relationships forgotten, as no one can remember place names or dates and so on. We are frustrated by the lack of an image-referencing system with details applicable to our lives. People forget. Talking in response to photographs means that the who, what, when, where, why, and how; the information behind the photographs is recorded. The people, places, and objects that are linked to the heritage of the narrator are invoked for posterity and descendants.

Documenting and Using Photographs and Objects to be Copied

- Always try to use a copy of a photograph rather than handle the original. Apart from the fact that it belongs to the narrator, the original may be fragile. Most computers and smart phones are able to scan photos for *copying* and digital filing. As well, photographs can be scanned by photocopiers. A more expensive option is to use professional photographic services. Portable scanners, some of which are capable of scanning objects as well as images, are excellent if you are at the narrator's home, for example, and would rather not or can't take the photograph away for scanning.

- If you need to take photographs and objects away for copying, make a list which serves as a receipt.
- Establish and integrate a classification system that links the image to the interview as soon as possible before the details are forgotten or confused.
- Note if a photograph has been altered in any way, for example: circled faces, arrows, names and dates scratched on the surface of the photograph.
- Note and ask about any writing found on the back of the photograph.
- Note time and date stamps for digital images.
- If the photograph has been taken professionally, note the photographer's name and/or business details.
- Ask if the narrator knows who took the photograph, the event or circumstances surrounding the image, the date the photo was taken, and who or what is in the photograph. Ask about any known specific stories surrounding the photo.
- Note the country and location of the photograph.
- Note whether the photo is black and white, colour, sepia, its dimensions, and whether or not a negative is available.
- Try to select clear, high-quality images wherever possible, but of course the narrative content of the photograph is far more important than its physical quality.
- If you take photographs of narrator objects try to use a camera capable of taking high-quality images such as a digital SLR camera. The amount of detail that a camera captures is called resolution. Resolution is measured in pixels. The more pixels a camera has the more detail it can capture.

Photographs and Permissions

- Always get formal, written permission to use and/or take photographs with the agreement written into the release documentation.
- Abide by copyright *restrictions* applying to the use of images. Copyright varies according to the country in which the oral history project is conducted.

- Many sites offer images under free Creative Commons licenses. Under these licenses, creators put their photographs online and specify how they can be used.

Digital Storytelling

A digital story recreates the practise of traditional storytelling using new media and digital video technology. A first-person narrative is made into a mini movie. Easy and often free and pre-loaded computer software is used to create the short movie. Making a digital story does not require expensive equipment, complicated software, or audio-visual editing skills. Apart from personal narratives the genre is useful for briefly examining themes and events, for delivering instructional content, or for giving an easily accessible overview of a topic.

Digital storytelling combines the art of telling stories with a mixture of digital graphics, text, recorded audio narration which publishes as a voiceover, video and or photographs, and music and/or sound effects to present the story or sometimes, specific information. "Classic" digital stories usually last for two to three minutes and are based, when using still images, on about a dozen photographs and a script of about 250 words. However, when making a digital story there are no specific rules regarding length, and the finished movie can be shorter or longer. Digital storytelling technology does not restrict users to a specific duration or impose limits on the number of images or words, but different software may have inbuilt limitations, such as the number of minutes a voice-over will play, for example. Professionals in the field of digital storytelling suggest that a shorter production is more effective and appealing for an audience.

Digital storytelling is an ideal method to seamlessly blend, coordinate, and store the significant and illustrative associated material often gathered when doing an oral history, such as photographs, traditional music, and artefacts and objects photographed for a digital story.

Creating a digital story relies on the use of images and music, so everyone involved in the making of a digital story must take care to abide by the relevant copyright rules. The safest way to be copyright compliant is to use photographs and or video taken and owned by the narrator. The same applies for music. A digital story, when used in an oral history context, creates a unique, personal narrative so images and music that belong to the narrator or which are easy to gain permission to use, such as family photographs, are apt. Original, copyright-free music is more problematic, as most of us have taken and own personal photographs but we can't all make music. There may be community recordings which are copyright free or for which permission can be sought. Classical music originating from the home country may be copyright free because copyright lapses after a period of time, depending on the country. You must always check. Otherwise, carefully source images, video, and music from reputable online libraries that offer copyright-free material.

Digital Storytelling: Three Approaches for Immigrant Oral Histories

1. A Short Narrative

Digital storytelling is an ideal platform to publish personal historical narrative as a summarized examination of personal historical themes and events. The integration of multimedia supports and enhances the recorded short history. The narrator has to be very selective about the narrative; the medium doesn't support a life history. Difficult content can be made more understandable because of the combined media approach. The narrator's voice is used to tell his or her own story as a synchronised voice-over, and the voice-over is supported by a combination of:

- Digital still photographs or other images or video (please note that not all digital story programs support the use of video)
- Scanned photographs and documents to support the digital story such as passport entries and birth certificates, citizenship certificates; anything which is relevant to the narrative
- Music which is supplied within the digital storytelling software. The advantage of inbuilt music is that there are no copyright restrictions. Selecting appropriate music can be time-consuming as there are hundreds of options, but the process of selection is enjoyable as it allows for creative interpretation. Otherwise, music is imported into the digital story. Abide by copyright restrictions applying to the use of music. Copyright varies according to the country in which the oral history project is conducted and may be difficult to understand, so take care
- Text captions, which are excellent if the narrator chooses to speak in a language other than English or if the narrator's accent is difficult to understand when speaking in English. This feature of digital storytelling has wonderful applications for immigrant narrators. They can be sure of saying exactly what they want to say in their first language with the

added advantage of a supplementary written, albeit brief, transcript in the first language and/or English

Because digital stories are short the narrator doesn't tire when narrating. Narrators can plan what they want to say, work cooperatively with someone who can help them with the English for their voice-over script, and practise what they plan to say multiple times. Narrators can do their voice-over without a script, if they choose, using the images they've selected and uploaded to the digital story to guide what they say. Some programs provide a text box for typing the story that's to be narrated.

2. Selected Sound Bites from an Oral History Recording

Digital storytelling is an ideal way to publish particular or salient aspects of an oral history recording; the digital story becomes representative of the full interview. A digital story also makes the full audio more accessible to a wider audience because of its comparative brevity and because a digital story file size suits a wider range of publishing platforms than the larger audio files of most oral history recordings. Digital stories take up far less space on websites and blogs, in social media and in e-mails, for example, than complete oral history recordings. In oral history, a sound bite is a short clip of speech extracted from the complete audio recording. A sound bite is chosen to capture the essence of the narrator's story. Ideally, listeners will be motivated to listen to the complete recording.

The difference between this approach and the first approach is that the narrator's voice-over is taken directly from a full oral history recording as a sound bite that is then coordinated to music and images within the digital story. In the first approach the narrator records directly onto the digital story program in response to uploaded images.

3. A Summary of a Community Multi-Narrator Oral History Project

A digital story is also a useful method to advertise an oral history project. Music significant to the immigrant community is easily included, as are maps and images such as flags and relevant stock photos. With this approach multiple sound bites are extracted from the different narrator recordings and matched to images and music. It's an excellent way to summarise an oral history project for a public viewing or to demonstrate the results of the project to commissioning bodies.[7]

Digital Storytelling Software Programs

There is a range of digital storytelling programs, many of which can be down-loaded for free. In addition, there are excellent free support sites. Free programs for PCs include Microsoft Photo Story 3,[8] a digital storytelling program that uses still photographs, and Microsoft Movie Maker. An advantage of Microsoft Movie Maker is that it allows the inclusion of video footage. For Apple computers, iMovie is an easy-to-use option that allows the use of both video and still images. Digital storytelling software comes with easy-to-follow guides on how to use the programs. As well, there are hundreds of Internet text guides and instructional YouTube videos that demonstrate how to use the various programs.

A digital story can be copied onto a DVD and viewed on a DVD player and TV, projected via a data projector, or uploaded to a website to be viewed online as streaming video. Digital stories can also be uploaded to online video publishing sites such as YouTube or Vimeo. Once published, digital stories can be embedded in a website or blog. Digital storytelling software allows numerous saving options. Probably the best option for a user is to save the story the same way it will be used or played.

Making a Digital Story

Creating a digital story requires a basic level of computer literacy. The necessary skills are certainly achievable for computer users who are comfortable using a computer in general. Novice computer users will probably appreciate some help with creating a story. Realistically, the first approach could be done by a narrator without assistance or with minimal assistance. Creating a digital story works well when a narrator is given help to make the digital story because the genre is conducive to collaboration. Digital storytelling is also a wonderful group activity. Digital stories following the second and third approach would be produced by the oral historian who has conducted an oral history and is familiar with creating sound bites using an audio editing program such as Audacity, Hindenburg Journalist, or Pro Tools, among others.

The basic steps in creating a digital story are:

1. Decide upon the narrative
2. Select photographs that support the chosen narrative
3. Create a voice-over script or prompts for narration

4. Follow the steps of the chosen software to create the digital story

Online step-by-step guides for creating digital stories number in the hundreds.

Video Oral Histories

A video oral history does not simply record the narrator's voice; facial expressions, hand gestures, mannerisms, and body language are recorded. Listeners see how the narrator looks as well as sounds. The setting of the film might add interest and detail to the oral history narrative if the filming is done in a location or environment pertinent to the narrator. Videoed narrative can be a particularly suitable approach for immigrant family oral histories because after the inevitable occurs, family members not only have an historical family record, but can also see their loved one telling the story.

The technical competency expected of the video interviewer has similarities to the requirements of audio oral history recording. The difference is that for videoed oral histories the interviewer has to know how to set up the physical interview setting for lighting as well as set up excellent sound. Good lighting is required in the room as well as on the narrator. The physical setting needs additional consideration because of its visibility to listeners and also because it may affect the narrative if the narrator doesn't feel comfortable or if the physical setting is inappropriate or not meaningful for them. For the narrator, film shots have to be composed following filming conventions to get good visual results such as centring the narrator's face so that the eyes are about one third from the top of the viewfinder or television screen. Setting up the audio-visual space requires more equipment and may also require a camera operator so that the interviewer can concentrate on the interview. For some narrators the additional paraphernalia of a video oral history may be intimidating. The approach might be particularly stressful for narrators who recount traumatic narrative. Depending on their circumstances narrators may feel uncomfortable about what to wear or how they look or simply dislike the idea of being filmed. A narrator may find it difficult to immerse themselves in telling their story in the less intimate setting of a videoed recording. Video recording doesn't allow for narrators who want anonymity.

Chapter 8

AN ORAL HISTORY PROJECT STEP BY STEP

"Every old man that dies is a library that burns."
—a proverb

The focus of oral history is on listening and collaborative creation between the narrator and the interviewer. It is a two-way activity. A narrator shares memories with an interviewer who has researched and planned the interview. Oral history project steps are developed as a partnership.

An oral history project with one or more people with an immigrant background follows the same steps as any oral history project except that the oral history interviewer or project coordinator must have engaged appropriately with the community significant to the narrator, allowed for pertinent cultural matters, planned for the possibility of trauma being a feature of the interview, and compensated for any English as a second language issues.

Oral history projects follow three general stages: Pre-Interview, Interview, and Post-Interview. Each stage requires careful thought, planning, and effort. An oral history project conducted effectively and skilfully is multifaceted and takes considerable time to complete successfully.

Pre-Interview

Step 1: Plan the Project Ethically

- Establish the project according to internationally recognised best practice for the ethical collection of oral history. National oral history associations provide comprehensive guidelines.[1]

- Scope the project in consultation with stakeholders such as the immigrant community, commissioning group, project committee or organisers, and individual narrators. Oral history projects vary in size so plan accordingly.
- Decide upon the project's focus, goals, and proposed outcomes.
- Consider and allow for legal issues relating to oral history. Determine who retains copyright of the interview. Adhere to copyright laws for images and associated material such as music used in a digital story or radio segment. Be careful about any situation that may affect the long-term viability of individual interviews or the overall project. Everyone involved with the project should have the same informed understanding and *informed consent* about the project, and this should be substantiated with clearly understood, plainly written, concise, and signed documentation. Unsigned release documentation drastically limits interview access.
- Plan for narrators who can't read English. Documentation can be translated by an interpreter if used, bilingual documents can be prepared in advance, and the interviewer can read or rephrase the documents for the narrator. For additional legitimacy record the reading or rephrasing of documentation for the narrator at the end of the audio interview.
- Plan for narrators who want to remain anonymous. Immigrant narrators who experienced political persecution, for example, may be unwilling to use real names, so establish systems to indicate a pseudonym has been used and safeguard anonymity.
- Create written documents for the project that will vary according to the project: equipment checklist, letter of introduction, pre-interview checklist, Release/Conditions of Use form, pre-interview questionnaires, generic project introduction and conclusion wording, typical but project-appropriate genealogical questions, interpreter instructions, annotated log templates, and thank-you letters.[2]
- Establish the parameters of topics that can and can't be addressed for each interview.
- Establish how interviews will be used and published, especially if the interview or parts of it will be published online, as online publication is ubiquitous.
- Determine the procedure you'll follow if a narrator says something *defamatory* or retells something inappropriate or illegal or reveals potentially illegal practices from the past. What will you do if it appears a narrator is telling lies or recalls narrative with a self-serving bias? What will

you do if you realise that the narrator is recounting a rehearsed script or you sense that the narrator is saying what they think you want to hear?

- Do not make promises you cannot keep. As an oral historian you cannot necessarily promise confidentiality about what is said in the interview. For example, there is always the possibility that a narrator may disclose criminal activity. Be mindful for everyone involved of legal responsibilities. Consider the ramifications of the Boston College Oral History Project case.[3]
- Account for the specific needs of child narrators, if their stories are to be collected for the project. Implement legal requirements such as parental and guardian consent, police checks, and working with children checks.[4]
- Explore the implications and organise for the needs of interviewing a narrator for whom English is not the first and most comfortable and authentic language in which to talk about the past.
- Ensure the project is conducted in a culturally appropriate manner.
- Make sure care is available, if needed, if trauma is a feature of the project.

Step 2: Make Allowances for the Nature of Memory

Memory isn't always reliable. Whose memory is the narrator retelling? Memories may be learned after the event through talking and listening, reading, movies and television, and from the Internet and other sources. Experience is subjective. It's normal for different people to have different recollections of history, of what happened in the past. This happens even if people were at the same place at the same time.

There are challenges and rewards when interviewing elderly narrators. They may recall events from the past with ease and great clarity but have difficulty remembering, for example, if they have already told you something; be patient.

Step 3: Organise a Pre-Interview

- Decide if the pre-interview will be conducted by phone or in person. Clarify as many dates, names, and spellings as you can during the pre-interview. For some English as second language users, an interview in person is the better option because speaking by phone doesn't allow clarification of information using body language and facial expressions. A face-to-face meeting is also more likely to allow as much time as the narrator needs to discuss the proposed interview.

- Gather information to guide and shape the interview and research. If preferred, the narrator can complete a written questionnaire.
- Discuss and clarify issues and concerns and establish boundaries for the interview—what will and can't be talked about.
- Work out the logistics regarding when and where the interview will take place. Discuss the interview space set-up to try to ensure optimal sound quality for the recording. Confirm that you and the narrator have the same perception of a space suitable for recording audio. Discuss unwanted noises: birds singing; dogs barking; babies crying; fridges humming; blinds flapping; paper shuffling; phones ringing and vibrating; clocks ticking; watches, rings, and bangles bumping; observers moving; pens tapping; and so on. Explain why as quiet a room as possible is important for the interview. If it seems a quiet space is unlikely, make the best arrangements possible.
- Arrange for the interview to occur wherever the narrator feels comfortable; often people choose to be interviewed at home or a familiar location such as a workplace.
- Organise for an interpreter if needed.
- Find out if other people will be present during the interview. Ideally an interview is best conducted with the interviewer and the narrator, but sometimes narrators like other people to be at the interview. Discuss with them how they should conduct themselves during the interview; for example, there should be minimal communication from additional people, as the interview relationship is between the interviewer and the narrator.
- Discuss the use of photographs and photographs of objects and other memorabilia to support the narrative—how they'll be used, copyright, and how to get photographs or copies for the project. Very clearly explain the legalities of copyright for images.
- Find out if you can take a photo of the narrator during the interview session or ask them to supply a photo. Interview logs and transcripts and websites with audio and other publication methods are enhanced by a picture of the narrator. It's nice to know what the person looks like both now and in the past as well, if possible.
- Talk about how long the narrator should allow for the interview. Explain that interview times vary, but about an hour for each interview session is a good benchmark. Long interviews can be problematic because the narrator may tire. Schedule additional sessions as needed.
- Explain that you have to allow extra time for setting up and packing up equipment and for completing required paperwork.

Step 4: Do Research on the Project

Carry out thorough research for the interview. You must know and understand as much as possible about the background impacting on the narrator's story. With proper research you are able to ask questions and follow leads appropriately. Some places for research include:

Traditional historical sources such as books, historical records, and documents
Museums and libraries
Images, photographs, videos and films, maps, and memorabilia
Buildings, sites, and locations
Government agencies
Historical societies
Family, friends, colleagues, and neighbours
Internet searches
Newspapers, journals, papers, and magazines

The pre-interview is an opportunity to learn about the narrator and the proposed interview.

Interview

Before the interview begins reassure the narrator. Explain the narrator's rights and go over the goals and plans for the interview. Discuss any concerns.

At the start of the recording, identify the interview in an organized, systematic method. Include the title of the project, the narrator's name, interviewer's name, the date, and location. If there is more than one interview, identify the interviews sequentially and use generic wording for consistency at the start of each interview. Include additional pertinent information such as if an interpreter was used, and include all the details including the interpreted language.[5]

Step 5: Set the Recording Format of the Digital Recorder

Use the internationally recognized standard for oral history recording: uncompressed 24/48 kHz WAV (24 bit/48 kilohertz Waveform Audio File Format). Don't record in MP3 compressed format as it is unsuitable for long-term preservation. Usually, interviewers set the recorder before going to the interview so that they can concentrate on the interview. Ideally, use power from an electrical outlet. Use batteries as a backup. Aim to get the best possible audio quality by becoming thoroughly conversant with your equipment and by practicing how to use it. External microphones are generally considered better for good sound quality than a recorder's inbuilt microphone.

Step 6: Decide on the Interview's Structure

Interviews develop depending on their purpose, and every interview is different. Remember the purpose of the interview. For life story interviews, following themes such as employment, interests, and family is generally more productive than a timeline approach, but follow a pattern which best suits the narrator and the interview.

Start with genealogical information to establish the interview and provide background. Then, for a project which has more than one narrator and a consistent theme, ask any questions that are common to all the interviews in the project. Next, ask questions specific to the individual narrator.

Step 7: During the Interview

- Set up the equipment—recorder, headphones, power cords, microphones and stands, and camera and scanner—beforehand. Have a box of tissues available in case the narrator becomes upset. Have water available. Make sure you have spare batteries.
- Do a sound check before the interview starts. Make sure all the equipment is working before you begin the interview.
- Consider having a second recorder of equal quality as backup.
- Record in as quiet an environment as possible. Close windows and doors if possible. Arrange for the interview to be conducted using two firm, stable chairs, ideally with a table on which to place equipment. A dining or kitchen setting is ideal. Cover the table with some sort of cloth, mat, or rug to absorb noise. Sit close to the narrator without invading the narrator's personal space. Position yourself so that eye contact is easily maintained. Explain to the narrator that you are listening to everything being said, but that occasionally you will be checking the equipment dials to ensure the volume and levels are correct. Avoid sitting on lounge or easy chairs because it is more difficult to maintain the required posture for a long significant conversation. Make sure your narrator is comfortable.

- Let the recorder run if there is an interruption. Deleting extraneous noise is simple with digital audio files and easier than cutting and pasting different audio files together. Plus, the audio quality will remain constant if you use one file for the entire interview. Establish protocols such as hand raising to pause the interview and signals for you as the interviewer to indicate if the narrator is inadvertently tapping the table, rocking the chair, moving away from the microphone, and so on. Turn off all cell phones. Cell phones can cause a hissing sound in some digital audio recorders even when they are on silent.
- Don't say "umm" and don't cross-talk or interrupt your narrator; wait until the narrator has finished speaking.
- Don't use meaningless utterances in the interview such as questions beginning with "and," "well," "like," and "so" and responses such as "gosh," "wow," "uh huh," "oh no," "no way," "cool," "really," "goodness," and so on. In general conversation these phrases are acceptable; but during an interview they are extremely annoying for listeners. Editing out the interjections is time-consuming and tiresome.
- Stop talking and listen intently and carefully. . . . Whose story is it? The interview's focus is the narrator, not the interviewer.
- Don't use swivel or wheeled chairs; they are invariably noisy. Check that the chairs you use don't squeak and that the table doesn't wobble.
- Position the microphones so they can't be knocked by the narrator or touched.
- Be highly observant about noise in the recording setting. Train yourself to be aware of noise not normally noticed. You may be fortunate enough to have a sound studio.
- Wear headphones—if you wear headphones you'll be able to pick up the sounds the microphones and recorder are picking up and that may affect the quality of the recording. In everyday life listeners tend to not notice peripheral noise such as a radio, people talking, an air conditioner turning on and off, and so on in the background, but audio recorders record every sound. As well, if you wear headphones you'll know immediately if the power has been accidently cut off to the recorder or if the microphone batteries have stopped working.
- Avoid paper noise during the interview. Use thin cardboard or firm, good quality paper that won't rustle when handled during the interview. Drop pages to the floor once you have finished with them rather than rearranging them during the interview.

Step 8: Questions and Prompts

The interview should focus on what the narrator knows rather than what you want to know. Consider whether you feel more comfortable with using questions or prompts or a combination. Prompts are similar to questions. The difference is that the interviewer formulates questions in situ. For example, rather than, "Where were you born?" the interviewer might simply write the word "birthplace" as a reminder to ask a question about birthplace. Whatever your choice, prepare questions or prompts for the interview based on your research and the pre-interview. Avoid published generic question lists as they do not usually allow for individuality. Regard the questions and prompts as a strong guide to help the interview stay on track. It's not possible to record everything. Questions and prompts are not meant to be followed slavishly. They provide a focus for the interview, but during the interview respond to what the narrator says and follow leads and topics as they arise. Go with the flow of the interview. The narrator is helped to recount and reflect on information and insights from the narrator's point of view on the specific topics and events intended for the interview. Prepared questions and prompts are invaluable in helping the interviewer ensure that the objectives of the oral history project are met as initially planned. However, an effective and perceptive oral historian also recognises that an interview may not go as planned and may in fact give unanticipated insights and information. Be flexible and prepared for the unexpected.

Begin the interview with relatively easy-to-answer questions about the narrator's genealogy—standard family information like the names of parents, grandparents, siblings, and relevant dates. This reassures the narrator that answering questions and participating in an interview is feasible and achievable. The questions gently prepare the narrator for questions that may be harder to answer. The genealogical information that is collected is valuable information for researchers and family historians. Gathering this information isn't mandatory, but it is useful.

- Ask open questions that encourage a comprehensive response as opposed to "yes/no" or limited fact answers.
- Don't suggest answers within questions. For example:
  "How terrible did you feel when you left your family?" The narrator might answer, for example, "Very terrible" and give no additional information. The question also suggests an answer that presumes the narrator felt terrible. The interviewer's presumption may not be true. The narrator might have been pleased to leave.

- Ask narrators to create descriptions in their "mind's eye" (though for unconfident second language narrators avoid this term) . . . "Can you take me on a tour of the house as you remember it, starting at the front door?" "Tell me about the people who lived in the street, house by house." "What did the city seem like when you were a child?"
- Listen carefully during the interview and respond appropriately. Pay attention. This is harder than you think because as well as participating in the interview, you have to ensure all the technical needs of the interview such as recording levels, volume, power supply, battery usage, lighting, and so on are being met.
- Attempt to pronounce proper nouns for narrator names and locations and other significant words the way they are pronounced by the narrator. This shows respect to the narrator. The pronunciations may be difficult. It is especially important to pronounce the narrator's name as correctly as possible. Some non-English names are very difficult to say, but practice the name and do your best. Some narrators will have adopted an "English" first name. If this is the case use the "English" name, but remember to record the first language name in the paperwork.
- Don't ask multiple response questions. A narrator who hears a question that requires many answers might respond to only one of the topics you've asked about. It's hard enough for most people to recall memories from the past in an interview setting without having to recall information on more than one idea or topic.
- Don't ask double negative questions. A double negative occurs when two forms of negation are used in the same sentence. The question becomes ambiguous. Double negative questions are very confusing to understand, especially for narrators engaging in a language in which they are not fully conversant. The narrator finds it hard to ascertain what the interviewer would like to know. The confusion is intensified in an interview setting because the narrator is concentrating hard and may feel under pressure because of the presence of microphones, recording equipment, and so on. An interview's setting is unlike a normal conversation where double negatives are tolerated. Even though in spoken English the use of double negatives is generally acceptable, in an interview, because the ultimate aim is to get a clear, accurate recount, double negatives should not be used. They sound reasonable but are not. Examples of double negative questions are:
  Did you not think that your town was unlikely to be targeted?
  Why didn't you not feel nervous when you did the test?

When the interview has finished
- Ask if there is anything the narrator would like to add or talk about.
- Take time at the end of your interview to gently wind down the interview as a mark of respect and consideration for the narrator. Talking about life experiences can be draining, arduous, challenging, and possibly confrontational, so the conclusion of an interview should not be abrupt. Time to chat, talk about what happened in the interview, and debrief is important. Sometimes after the recorder has been turned off, narrators may provide further information that should be noted, if permission is granted by the narrator in writing.
- If trauma has been a feature of the interview, follow appropriate procedures to care for everyone affected: the narrator and, possibly, yourself, as the interviewer, and companions and the interpreter if present.
- Complete the paperwork. A carefully considered and planned release form is essential and mandatory in order to be able to use and publish the interview in whatever form is intended. The release form should cover all aspects of copyright for the interview, including additional material supporting the interview, such as images, artefacts, and documents. The release form outlines copyright ownership of the interview. A list of any additional documentation gathered for the interview should be noted in writing. Confirm narrator contact details. The narrator should be fully conversant with copyright ownership in respect to what was said in the interview. The narrator needs to know how the narrator's words and the overall project will be used and any consequences. This is especially important if the interview will be published online.
- Write a brief summary/report as soon as possible after the interview. Note observations that may be useful for future reference. For example, was the narrator especially nervous about being interviewed, did the narrator ask for a companion to be present and who was the companion, were there interruptions and equipment fails such as battery replacements, unwanted noise—anything of interest that occurred during the interview that won't necessarily be covered in a transcription or annotated log.

Post-Interview

Step 9: Process the Interview

In oral history recording two distinct interview files are created:

1. The original WAV recording. This remains completely untouched; no alterations whatsoever are made. It is the archival file.
2. From the archival file copies in WAV or MP3 are made.
- Download the audio file to a computer.
- Use a sound editing program such as Audacity, Hindenburg Journalist, Pro Tools, or GarageBand for audio *processing*.
- Create a timed/annotated log and/or write a summary and/or create a transcript. A written record complements and supports the audio record and provides an opportunity to record in writing important factual information such as names and how they are spelled. A timed annotated log gives researchers and listeners relatively easy access to specific information they want to follow up in the recording. Summaries provide a brief account of the important aspects of the interview. Transcripts provide the most detailed record but are very time-consuming and not always the best option for interviews with narrators lacking English proficiency.
- Save the original recording in its entirety for archival storage in the originally recorded uncompressed 24/48 kHz WAV - 24 bit/48 kilohertz Waveform Audio File Format.
- Save the original recording at least three times and in different places: on a computer hard drive, an external hard drive, in cloud storage, on a private website, on a USB, a CD, or a DVD.
- Make copies of the original recording and edit for listener accessibility, such as topping and tailing of general chitchat at the start and end of the interview, and removal of unwanted noise and interruptions. Consider creating sound bites, small segments from the interview to illustrate the complete interview.
- Give the narrator a copy of the audio recording and associated paperwork to check for accuracy. At this stage the narrator may want to clarify what was said in the interview or possibly make changes.
- Plan for an audience. There is not much use in oral histories that don't get listened to or used in some form; they should be published. Convert the WAV file to MP3. MP3 is very useful for audio distribution and publication because of its relatively small file size.
- Publish the interview as requested and planned, for example: installations, displays, for audio tours, performances, books, articles, curriculum materials, radio shows, digital stories, in reminiscence therapy, websites, and in libraries and museums for research.

- Archive the interview according to agreements established by the commissioning agent. Follow repository guidelines.
- Give copies of the recording, associated paperwork, and publication genre to the narrator. Work with them on launches and displays. Celebrate with them the joint creation of a wonderful achievement, a historical record. Thank them.

Chapter 9

SAVAN – A CASE STUDY WITH AN IMMIGRANT NARRATOR

"I so lucky."[1]

Savan's Story

Savan Hin was born in Cambodia in the province of Kampot, south of the capital, Phnom Penh, on February 6, 1946. Savan referred to herself as an orphan, a "kamprea"—orphan in Khmer, Cambodia's national language. Savan's mother, Ran Sot, died when she was a day old. Her biological father, Yen Kim, left Savan in the care of her grandmother, Bun, and grandfather, Sot Bor.

Yen Kim and Savan's mother divorced when Savan's mother was three months pregnant. Yen Kim married another woman. Following Cambodian custom after divorce or death, Yen Kim's new wife did not take on the responsibility of care of children from a prior relationship. Savan was an only child but she lived with three female cousins, close to her in age, cared for as well by her grandparents because their mother had died and their father had remarried. Both her grandparents were rice farmers and very poor.

Savan's mother had remarried when she was pregnant with Savan, and Savan thought of her mother's second husband as another father. His name was San Hin and he had loved her mother, Ran Sot, dearly.

As a child Savan learned how to manage a home by observing her grandmother cooking, washing, cleaning, and working on the farm. Her biological father did not visit her, and her grandparents, especially her grandmother, took full responsibility for her upbringing. When Savan was a baby

Figure 9.1: Savan, Sydney, NSW. Photo courtesy Savan Hin.

her grandmother found a nursing mother for her so that she could have milk each day, and at night she fed her porridge. This was all very difficult for Bun. Later, after one of Savan's friends had pointed out who her father was, Savan saw him every day when he drove his horse and cart taxi to the local market.

Despite her grandparents' poverty, Savan went to Primary (Elementary) school for five years from ten years of age until she was fifteen in 1961. She was a gifted student, excelled at school, and was given gifts from relatives to help her continue her studies. Savan loved to study so she stayed on at school to continue learning even though she had finished her elementary education after about four years. The school was a local village school run by Buddhist monks in a Buddhist monastery. The monks were trained teachers and taught standard curriculum but no religious instruction. Her cousins did not go to school because of their home duties and lack of financial support from relatives, but Savan, an only child and identifiably clever, was able to attend school.

In 1963 San Hin found out that Savan could not access Secondary (High School) education. In 1965 he arranged for her to move to Phnom Penh to live with him to further her education. Savan moved to the capital and lived with San Hin but didn't attend school because she found city life overwhelming and she was too scared to go to a city school. Instead, Savan helped her second father's third wife, a doctor in a hospital in Phnom Penh, with her three children and home duties. Savan later left Phnom Penh for Battambang to live with her "brother" Sophann Hin, San Hin's son from his first marriage. In Battambang she looked after Sophann's children. Battambang is near the city of Siem Reap in northwestern Cambodia and close to the border with Thailand.

After meeting Yauth Mauv in Battambang, Savan married him in 1969. Her husband was a trained teacher and had been a Buddhist monk and he was also a rice farmer. As well, Yauth did translation work for tourists at the Angkor Wat archaeological site, the Siem Reap temple complex, which is the largest religious monument in the world. Savan and Yauth lived with Yauth's father who also had care of the two children, Yet (male) and Yar (female) Mauv from Yauth's first marriage.

Savan's only son, Vendredi (named after French for Friday because he was born on a Friday) was born in 1970. Savan discovered that the name Vendredi confused people, so most Cambodian people called Savan's son Sovong. In Australia Vendredi/Sovong was anglicised to Sean. The political situation in Cambodia at that time was horrific because of the Cambodian five-year civil war of 1970–1975, but Savan's life at that time was described by her as normal. As part of the Vietnam War effort American planes bombed Cambodia on an immense scale. Devastation was widespread and affected thousands of Cambodians. The bombing of Cambodia targeted enemy troops hiding in Cambodia. U.S. and South Vietnamese soldiers infiltrated the same region to eradicate the enemy—North Vietnamese and Viet Cong troops.[2] None of this affected Savan and her family. Savan described her situation as lucky as she lived near the border with Thailand rather than Vietnam where the bombing occurred. Savan was aware of what was happening, but it didn't affect her daily life.

Savan's life changed dramatically in 1975, as did the lives of millions of Cambodians. Pol Pot, leader of the Khmer Rouge, declared Year Zero for Cambodia, also known as Democratic Kampuchea, and implemented a communist dictatorship that imposed radical agrarian socialism. Pol Pot and the Khmer Rouge troops captured Phnom Penh on April 17, 1975. Almost immediately Pol Pot started to implement his plan to transform Cambodia into a communist peasant farming society. The Khmer Rouge plan relied on forcibly evacuating Cambodian people at gunpoint from cities and villages to the rural area from which they originally came, and this occurred as soon as the Khmer Rouge came to power. Intelligentsia and people such as civil servants, Buddhist monks, ex-army members, and professionals were "eliminated" to ensure a pure new Cambodian society without stimuli from the past. Foreigners were expelled, as were foreign influences such as languages other than Khmer, international business, and support. Money was taken out of circulation. Embassies were closed.[3]

Throughout her interview, when Savan talked about her personal experiences from April 1975 until January 1979, she always referred to Pol Pot as if she saw him personally implement atrocities and deprivations. Savan always said that Pol Pot did this or that when she was actually referring to the actions of Khmer Rouge implementers. The Khmer Rouge had male and female followers.

Millions of Cambodians were moved from their homes in cities and villages. Savan remembers that the Khmer Rouge troops said, "Leave, leave, leave."[4] Savan, Yauth, and Sovong were living at Poy Pet on the border of Thailand. Savan's husband had just built a house in 1973 at Poy Pet for a building business he had established there. Savan, Yauth, and Sovong were forced to travel by foot back to Battambang to their "real place"—the place Savan's family had initially lived before in Cambodia. For Savan this was Phum Omony, where her husband was born. During the forced evacuation Savan's waist-length hair was cut short with Yauth's razor. Savan and Yauth were told that young women (Savan was about twenty-eight years old) with long hair would have their throats cut with a sugar palm frond by Khmer Rouge troops. Terrified for his wife's life, Yauth cut Savan's hair very short. She said it looked terrible.

During the forced evacuation Savan remembers that poor people survived more often than wealthy evacuees. Poor people took food and clothing with them for the forced walk, whereas wealthy people took cash, which was of no use because the Khmer Rouge devalued money.

At the time that Savan, her husband, and son were forced to leave Poy Pet, Savan's grandparents were living at Phum Somrong Krome. They were not forced to evacuate because the suburb of Somrong Krome was already communist controlled. As for her other relatives and friends, she was unaware of what had happened to them or where they were sent by the Khmer Rouge because everyone was separated. People didn't know what was happening to others.

From Phum Omony Savan was evacuated again, this time to isolated bush in the countryside where she ended up working in rice fields Yauth owned. This made the second evacuation for Savan and her family less traumatic because they went to a familiar area, fields they owned and knew. They travelled about five kilometres. The fact that they owned the land she was forced to farm by the Khmer Rouge was kept secret—"we don't say anything—must to ignore."[5] Savan's husband was twice taken to be executed, because previously, in 1971 and 1972, he had joined the Cambodian government army opposing Pol Pot and the Khmer Rouge. Yauth avoided execution because on the register Pol Pot used to identify people's occupations, Savan always insisted that her husband was a rice farmer rather than a teacher and soldier. The register identified people to be killed according to occupations that did not suit the new regime. Savan referred to the register as a census.

At first in 1975 Savan, Yauth, and Sovong lived together. Later, the family, following Khmer Rouge policy, was separated. Savan worked in the rice fields and Yauth worked as a chef. They lived apart. Sovong, five years old, wasn't separated from his parents and sent to a children's collective because he was small and thin and looked a lot younger than his age, so he avoided living in a large, separate children's group. He lived with his father. Despite Savan working in rice fields and Yauth working as a chef, there was no additional food whatsoever. The Khmer Rouge strictly forbade this. Meals were communal. Savan ate twice a day—at lunch and dinner. For about the first two months people were given enough rice, but after that for every meal people ate rice porridge—two cans of rice into a very large pot of water with no vegetables and very occasionally a small amount of meat. This was the food allowance for more than four years. Sometimes Pol Pot's people would kill a cow and this would be shared, but most of the meat was eaten by Khmer Rouge members. Occasionally Yauth caught fish which he gave to Savan and Sovong. He could do this if he was given a night job and was able to surreptitiously fish for the extra food even though fishing was strictly forbidden. This meant that Savan occasionally received extra nourishment and that she did not have to steal food, which was punishable by death. Malnourishment caused Savan and the other Cambodian women she knew to stop menstruating and to lose breast tissue. Savan worked from 3 A.M. until 8 P.M. every day and walked to and from the fields in the dark. Her eyesight was adversely affected by her heavy workload and starvation-level diet, and Savan lost her ability to navigate in the dark. She lived in a shelter made from coconut and palm leaves without proper walls. There was no effective medicine—Savan and everyone she knew called the medicine they were given by the Khmer Rouge "rabbit poo" because it was not real medicine and was made from rice flour. Many people got sick. The monasteries and schools were used as hospitals, but the treatment given in the hospitals to ordinary Cambodians was completely ineffective.

Pol Pot's people tested everyone to see if they were educated. Savan tricked the Khmer Rouge by writing with her left hand even though she was right-handed. Writing with her left hand made her appear to have no expertise in writing and therefore uneducated.

Spying by children was also a fact of life (kang chhlop).[6] Relationships that developed between men and women were forbidden unless they were authorised by the Khmer Rouge. A Cambodian female friend of Savan, also living in Australia, had been forced to marry a Pol Pot man. Spies reported on illicit romantic liaisons. If a couple was caught they were killed the same day after being given a special meal at 5 P.M. A man's liver and heart were removed and Savan heard that the heart and liver were sometimes eaten by Khmer Rouge people. Savan also heard that if the woman was pregnant the baby was removed from the corpse. The sign the couple would die was the special meal. Savan says this was done to warn others to do as the Khmer Rouge said. Savan was always terrified of ghosts returning from the people who were killed. When recalling her fear of ghosts during her interview, Savan jumped when she heard a car horn used outside. Savan did not ever see someone killed, but she was a regular witness to people who had died because of overwork, starvation, or execution. Leaving her village she saw the body of a man with his hands and legs tied and his eviscerated stomach stuffed with grass.

On January 7, 1979, Vietnamese troops captured Cambodia's capital and stopped the murderous regime of Pol Pot and the Khmer Rouge. A moderate Communist government was established and Pol Pot and the Khmer Rouge were removed from control of Cambodia.[7] With other Cambodians Savan and her family escaped from the rice fields when the Khmer Rouge abandoned their responsibilities after they learned Pol Pot had lost control. Savan and her family walked to the Thai border and lived there for a few months.

The Red Cross arranged for buses to take Cambodians seeking refuge to Thailand. Savan and her husband and son went to the Khao-I-Dang Holding Center refugee camp on the Thai-Cambodian border located twenty kilometres north of Aranyaprathet in Prachinburi, now Sakeo Province. In 1980 at Khao-I-Dang, Savan and Yauth started a business selling baskets made from bamboo to an American supplier. This lasted for about five months. Teachers were needed in the camp so Yauth applied and was accepted then later Savan also started working as a teacher of children aged eight to fifteen years old. Savan remembered how she had been taught in Cambodia and followed that pattern of tuition. She was a popular and highly competent teacher who was loved and respected by students and supervisors. Savan was awarded a Teaching Certificate and trained student teachers as well as children. Savan was very proud of her Teaching Certificate.

They lived in Thai refugee camps for four years until 1983; Khao-I-Dang Holding Center refugee camp was home for two years. After that the family was in Kam Put camp until Savan, Yauth, and Sovong were accepted by Australia's Department of Immigration in 1983 as special refugees. Before leaving for Australia they were in Chonburi camp. Savan and Yauth were so overjoyed about their acceptance to live in Australia they inadvertently left behind their Teaching Certificates. This continues to cause Savan great regret. In Australia she was told she could apply to have her overseas qualifications considered for recognition but could not do so because the evidence was lost.

Savan started living in Australia in April 1983. Summarising her experiences under Pol Pot's genocidal rule, Savan always considered herself to be very lucky. She endured unthinkable daily horror, fear, and privations for over four years, but during her interview frequently explained the particular circumstances and events of her time living under Pol Pot's leadership as "lucky." After her interview I asked Savan if she had ever gone back to Cambodia. She said no because Cambodia was bad luck for her. Conducting the interview was a humbling experience for me as the interviewer, and I was impressed by Savan's courage and tenacity. That is one aspect of many refugee interviews that recurs; the amazing stoicism of the narrators.

Savan as a Narrator

I met Savan when she was a student in one of my Adult Education Language, Literacy, and Numeracy classes in Sydney, Australia in 2011. I love teaching these classes. Adult LLN classes are exceptionally rewarding because students attending them are invariably dedicated and determined to make life better by improving their English competence. The major focus of Adult Education Language, Literacy, and Numeracy classes in Australia is to help students not only become better English users but also prepare them for further education and training that leads to employment or help them with the English literacy requirements of current employment. Savan was a typical adult LLN student; she was enthusiastic, hardworking, and a joy to have in the class.

Background to the Interview

In 2009 I conducted a large oral history project based on the lives of many of my adult students, teachers, and staff where I worked and converted the oral histories into Literacy and Language learning materials designed to improve basic, essential skills. The lesson resources were published online, and I often used them to engage my students in their learning journey. Students learn best when they can identify with lesson content, so I found that my students loved improving their literacy skills using material based on personal histories they could relate to. The oral histories I had collected for the project were linked to well-known history such as the Vietnam War, World War II, Middle Eastern conflict, historical icons, and so on. Savan understood that I had the capacity to collect personal histories, and she became interested in telling her history to me. Savan understood that her story was important and significant, and she wanted to share and preserve it in audio format. Everyone's story is important. Savan Hin's story was more than personal and family; she experienced life during a universally recognised terrible historical period and could potentially add to what we know about life during Pol Pot's Khmer Rouge leadership in Cambodia.

Living in Cambodia during Pol Pot's control has been compared to the atrocities of Hitler. Estimates vary but up to a quarter of Cambodia's population of around 8 million died during the period Pol Pot and the Khmer Rouge had control of the country.[8] Savan, like so many other Cambodians, lost contact with family and friends. As her teacher I knew she was an avid user of social media partly in an effort to possibly regain contact with familiar Cambodians who were settled elsewhere in the world as, initially, humanitarian refugees or in Cambodia. I suggested to Savan that her oral testimony, placed on social media, as well as being preserved for future generations, might enhance her capacity to find lost people important to her.

It may seem ironic that an adult student of language and literacy would countenance telling unique personal history orally rather than use newly developing writing skills. However the reality is that to gain proficiency for new Language and Literacy users such as Savan, with a second language background, is very difficult. Language skills, especially expert control over writing, are very hard to achieve. Savan is an intelligent person and a former teacher, but the shift in facility from one language to another is hard. Good written English is difficult to master. It was much easier for Savan to recount her story orally rather than in writing. Savan's first interview lasted one and a half hours and was the equivalent of approximately 12,000 words. Writing the history would have taken her an immensely longer amount of time and may, in actuality, have been too onerous to complete for an emerging writer of English.

As well, many adult language learners find gaining literacy proficiency especially difficult because they are adults with all the responsibilities of running a home, raising a family and looking after extended family, living in a new country with a different culture and the demands of making a living, and in many cases, dealing with past trauma. Children attend school five days a week for about six hours a day for up to thirteen years without the responsibilities of being an adult, but adults typically squeeze their literacy and language tuition, by necessity, into fewer tuition hours. Savan, for example, had lessons for sixteen hours per week over four days.

Savan was in her late sixties when I interviewed her. Some may question why Savan was in a comprehensive English language program many years after arriving in Australia. The answer is typical of many new immigrant arrivals of Savan's era—she had to make a living as well as look after her family in her new country and did not have time to devote to a consistent and thorough English language education. Savan accessed classes in Australia but not systematically. In Thailand she had attended rudimentary English classes that provided a very basic understanding of spoken and written English. When she arrived in Australia Savan became a full-time working mother; she worked from home as an industrial sewing outworker and then in factories for many years. Savan had the time to devote to learning English, especially in its written form, when she was established in her new country.

Khmer Language

For Cambodian language, Khmer speakers, there are additional challenges when developing proficiency in English as a second language. Khmer script is very different from the English phonemic alphabet. Khmer uses a syllabic alphabet. Syllabic alphabets use symbols for consonants and vowels and each consonant has a characteristic vowel which can be changed to another vowel or muted with a diacritical mark. Vowels can also be written with separate letters when they occur at the start of a word or on their own. The English alphabet has five vowels and twenty-one consonants compared to Khmer's thirty-three consonants and more than twenty vowels. In Khmer text there are no spaces between words; spaces are used instead to show the end of a section or sentence. Spelling is not universally standardized; words can be spelled more than one way. This occurs in English spelling as well but not regularly—For example: jail/gaol, program/programme, and color/colour, but most English spelling is consistent. Savan frequently checked and adjusted Khmer spellings used in the interview in our post-interview discussions.

The Interview Process

Pre-interview: I met with Savan in person, rather than use the telephone to conduct the pre-interview. A phone interview would not have allowed me to clarify information given by Savan to mutually shape the interview. Savan's spoken English facility was not perfect; her pronunciation and oral discourse were not consistently regular. Savan's speech was difficult to understand if just one attempt was made to listen. A phone interview would not have allowed us to revisit comments that were made to ascertain exactly what was said. Also, Savan does not like speaking on the phone because without reference to facial features, body language, and prompts for clarification, she is usually unsure of the exact conversation. Oral history is individualised history but even so, the personal view of history recorded should be accurate, and for narrators for whom English is not the first language this is very important. As her teacher I knew Savan and had communicated with her often, but regardless of our familiarity I had to listen very carefully to her testimony to know exactly what she was saying; even then I did not understand everything she said without clarification in post-interview sessions.

Interviewer Preparation

For the interview I researched Cambodian history in general and specifically I studied the political and social situation in Cambodia when Savan lived there, paying particular attention to the Pol Pot era. I also researched information about Cambodian family relationships because I was aware from the pre-interview that Savan's family arrangements in Cambodia differed from those I was familiar with in Australia. For example, Savan considered herself an orphan even though she had both a living biological father and a second father—the man who had married her mother six months before she died and who obviously cared very much for Savan and took a significant interest in her welfare. I established through research that Savan's situation was typical for a Cambodian person and the concept of orphan is different in Cambodian culture from Australian culture, for example. An Australian orphan has no parents. A child with parents but under different adult care is considered another way. Even though the focus of the oral history recording was Savan's life in Cambodia, accuracy for the genealogical information typically gathered at the start of any interview had significant importance in this interview because Savan's information might possibly help locate missing relatives and friends. When Savan spoke sadly about leaving behind her Teaching Certificate and how she could have potentially had her qualifications recognised in Australia I had sufficient technical knowledge, because of my work as an adult educator, to understand the significance of her loss. I also renewed my understanding of Buddhism, Savan's first religion, and Christianity, the religion Savan accepted in Australia. Otherwise, all preparation for the interview followed standard procedure.

The Interview

Savan's interview took longer than I normally allow for an interview. It was conducted slowly. I spoke with less speed than usual so I could be sure she understood my questions and so I could confirm what she told me. Savan's accent was difficult at times to understand especially as she was retelling information for which I had no background knowledge apart from my research and past media reports. I spoke slowly but not so slowly as to be condescending and patronizing. In my experience second language users of English are insulted when spoken to very slowly. My phrasing followed normal spoken English patterns; I did not speak word by word which is sometimes misconstrued as a means of making spoken English easier to understand. I had a prepared list of questions and prompts that we deviated from where needed to accommodate Savan's oral history. I tried to pronounce Cambodian proper nouns as Savan pronounced them.

The family questions at the start of the interview were particularly important because of Cambodia's violent circumstances. These questions had a threefold purpose: a gentle easing into the interview's primary purpose— to preserve Savan's history; information for genealogical researchers in the future; and most importantly, an opportunity for current genealogical and friends and acquaintances research. In general I found Savan's family history complex and had to seek her assistance during the interview to clarify my understanding of her family members and their relationships to each other.

During the interview Savan varied her use of last (surname/family) then first (Christian/given) name Khmer format with the English format of first then last name. For this reason I wrote all names in first / last format in the summary of the interview. Savan didn't mind how names were conveyed.

I used a map of Cambodia during the interview to help me be clear about locations Savan mentioned. Savan's history included forced evacuations and migration within Cambodia so correct geography was essential. Savan helpfully wrote down some locations she wanted recorded but even so this remained problematic because as a non-Khmer speaker and writer I found the written information challenging; place names, as well as being unfamiliar, were long and I was unable to break down the structure of the addresses without assistance. Nor could I identify any names apart from Kampot and Battambang on maps. I was unable to understand Savan's explanations of the locations, and in an effort to be helpful she made some minor spelling adjustments! Savan's two locations written out to help me for the interview are as follows:

1. Phum Somrong Krome Khum Tramsorsor Srok Bunteaymeas Ket Kampot (Savan explained that Pol Pot renamed the location: Phum Somrong Khum Somrong Krome Srok Bunteaymeas Ket Kampot.)
2. Phum Omony Khum Anlongvile Srok Sanker Ket Battambang

Location 1 was for the first fifteen years of Savan's life from her birth in 1946 until 1962. In 1963 she went to live in the capital Phnom Penh. Location 2 is where Yauth first lived. Location 2 is where Savan met her husband in 1967 and lived until 1969.

Not until our post-interview discussion was I sure about the localities in Cambodia that Savan mentioned in her interview and had written down in English.

Phum Somrong Krome and Phum Omony – suburbs Somrong Krome and Omony

Khum Tramsorsor and Khum Anlongvile Srok Sanker – hamlet/shire/ region/area Tramsorsor and Alongvile Srok Sanker

Srok Bunteaymeas and Srok Sanker – Bunteaymeas district and Srok district

Ket Kampot and Ket Battambang – Kampot province and Battambang province

Easy when you're told how!

Why Didn't We Use an Interpreter?

The most preclusive factor was cost. Interpreter costs were well beyond the means of our project. In our favour was time; I had the time to conduct the entire interview process relatively slowly. Logistically I was able to see Savan a number of times after the recorded interview to clarify anything that was unclear because of Savan's lack of English language proficiency.

Interview Questions

Savan's interview questions are as follows. Although the questions were based on a pre-interview session, I adapted them as needed and did not follow them strictly.

Savan, could you please tell me your full name and spell it please.
When and where were you born?
What were your parents' names?
Where was your mother born and when?
Where was your father born and when?
Where did your parents meet and marry?
Please tell me about your grandparents.
What are the names of your brothers and sisters?
Cousins?
What is your husband's name?
What is your son's name?
Where was your son born?
What languages do you speak?
What is your first language?
Please tell me about your childhood in Cambodia.
Did you go to school?
Can you tell me about that please?
What happened in your life after you went to live with your real grandfather?
Tell me how you moved from Phnom Penh to Battambang.
Tell me about your early married life.
What was the political situation in Cambodia?
What was it like to live in Cambodia with Pol Pot as leader of Democratic Kampuchea?
Where did you go after leaving Cambodia?

When did you come to Australia?

Is there anything more you would like to add?

Vocabulary

When I asked Savan about her childhood she did not know what I was asking about. Instead I rephrased my question to "When you were a little girl . . ." Savan spoke of "milar," which from the interview context I understood to be malaria. When referring to the practice of Khmer Rouge soldiers hitting people on the back of the head with a shovel[9] before dropping them into graves, she did not know the word for shovel during the interview but in the first post-interview discussion she said she did, in fact, know the word shovel. Savan used the word "ashamed" when she described the misplacement of her Cambodian Teaching Certificate. From the context of the interview it was obvious that she was not in fact ashamed, rather she was sad and regretful. I had to repeat the word "safe" until she understood what I meant. In post-interview discussion I referred to Pol Pot as evil and I needed to explain the meaning of the word to Savan. When Savan talked about evacuation she used the term "countryside" rather than the more familiar term "rural" used in Australia. Savan described herself as being "lucky"; the word "luck" seemed inappropriate for describing situations that allowed a greater chance to stay alive. When speaking about her husband's niece, Savan said "his nephew is woman."[10] Several times Savan made errors with noun/pronoun agreement. There were other examples as well. Clarifying what we both meant extended the length of the interview and post-interview sessions but was vitally important.

Listening to a Firsthand Account of Evil and Trauma

Savan witnessed evil. Listening to her recounting evil and its consequences for her life was distressing for me as a listener and hard to grasp and comprehend because it was so terrible. In such circumstances it is crucial that the interviewer is sensitive to the needs of the narrator recounting the horror endured. Savan felt that in telling what happened to her, she in some way authenticated and validated what she experienced. She told me, with all my associated credentials, paperwork, equipment, and meetings, and I not only listened to her—her story was recorded and also fashioned into written documents designed to keep her story as a record others could read. An oral history interviewer must listen to the horror they hear with respect to their narrator and be thoroughly and thoughtfully prepared. I was compassionate but professional and this allowed the interview to proceed smoothly. Thorough research of the era was vital. Some of the evil and privations Savan described as "normal" would have seemed too appalling to believe had I not researched the Pol Pot era. Sadly, the horrors Savan described are widely documented in mainstream history references of the historical era she witnessed and survived, so I was mentally prepared for her likely experiences. Even so, in her interview and post-interview sessions, Savan seemed to sense that the terrors she described were hard for people who hadn't been through what she had experienced to accept, and the tone of her voice was insistent that what she witnessed and knew had happened was true.

Savan's interview focused on a period of her life approximately forty years previous to the interview. The trauma of that period of her life was not forgotten, but she did not appear unduly distressed in the interview. In fact, she told me often that telling her story made her happy and several times she told me that she "loved" the whole process. I gained the impression from her use of the word "loved" that Savan meant appreciation and gratitude rather than fondness and affection. She benefitted from telling her history and found the experience liberating. Nonetheless, as part of the interview procedures I reminded Savan about the support she had from her husband Yauth and her access to trusted mentors at her church. Savan also could have easily and freely accessed professional counselling services from a qualified psychologist had she wanted to, and I reminded her of this. I am an oral historian and a teacher; I am not a trained psychiatrist, psychologist, or psychotherapist, so I ensured Savan had and has future access to appropriate psychological support should she need it. Savan took the time to write an explanation as to why she felt at ease and peaceful despite the horrors and ordeal she had endured in Cambodia and why she did not suffer continued trauma from her time living under Pol Pot's rule.

"My new life in Australia

Since I came to know God, my life has changed. I never think about what happened in the past, I am always thinking about God (Jesus) first in my mind. Sometimes I have a problem, so I always pray to God for help. . . . I realise God loves me and he always stays with me."

Post-Interviews

Three formal post-interviews, one of two hours then two of thirty minutes, were conducted face-to-face. Together we slowly read through the summary I made of Savan's interview, ensuring there was ample time to confirm and clarify information. Usually I would do this by phone or in writing such as in an e-mail. As well as reviewing her summary and annotated log, Savan also reviewed this entire chapter as she is the focus. I explained difficult vocabulary to her. As well as meeting specifically for post-interview discussions, several times I briefly confirmed information with Savan face-to-face.

Savan seemed to view the entire interview process positively. When discussing the written documents of her audio interview, Savan made it clear that the history being written about was her story and she even negotiated photograph choice and placement and the most appropriate last paragraph. Savan very proudly gave a copy of her summary to every member of her church congregation.

Summary and Log versus Transcription

For Savan's interview a comprehensive summary and annotated log proved a better option than a transcription because Savan's spoken English was not consistently grammatically regular and sometimes hard to understand. A traditional transcription would not have resulted in an easy-to-read document nor an account that necessarily genuinely reflected Savan's testimony. The summary and annotated log, which included information from post-interview meetings, enabled processing of the interview to truly reflect the history Savan told. Transcription vagaries are well known. Narrators don't speak in sentence formats that transfer seamlessly to correct written English sentences. Spoken and written speech differs. When talking, speakers repeat themselves, mumble, stumble over words, leave out punctuation, forget to finish words and ideas, and lose the thread of what they are saying, amongst other foibles. Also, a transcription doesn't impart voice tone and body language. The transcriber can add comments such as "narrator appeared angry/comment was sarcastic in tone/narrator started crying" and so on depending on the interview, but it is not as accurate and real as listening to the interview. Transcription issues are compounded when the narrator does not have full control over the language used in the interview, in Savan's case, spoken English.

For researchers the summary, annotated log, and the audio file provide ample material for study.

APPENDIX A: ORAL HISTORY PROJECT WRITTEN RELEASE / CONDITIONS OF USE FORM

Narrator: _____

Interviewer: _____

Date and place of interview: _____

_____ would like your permission to use spoken, written, and graphic material collected from you for this oral history project. The material may be used wholly or in part. The interviews and any accompanying materials may be used in the future to produce written documents such as transcripts/partial transcripts, annotated logs, summaries, articles, curriculum materials, books, scripts, promotions for the project., and so on. They may be made into digital productions such as digital stories, PowerPoints, slide presentations, videos and so on. They may be used in presentations such as installations, talks, and lectures. They may be used on websites. We are asking you for your permission to possibly edit, reproduce, publish, broadcast, transmit, perform, or adapt your interview. As a matter of courtesy you will be advised how your interview is used.

The project will be archived at _____

You own the copyright of your recorded interview. You can use your interview any way whatsoever. The same applies to written and graphic material collected from you to support this oral history project.

We also need to know if you would like any conditions of use placed upon your interview. For example, you may want to use a pseudonym, ask for content to be removed, restrict publication, and so on.

I give permission for my recorded interview and accompanying written and graphic material to be used for _____ oral history project according to the above description.

Would you like any condition(s) placed upon your interview?
Please circle   No   Yes

If Yes, please explain your condition(s). PTO if needed and sign and date the page.

Signature of narrator _____

Date _____

Address _____

Zip code/Postcode _____

E-mail address _____

Phones: Home _____ Work _____
Cell/Mobile _____

Signature of Interviewer _____ Date _____

Interviewer contact details _____

APPENDIX B: PROJECT DETAILS, FIELD NOTES, AND ANNOTATED LOG

```
┌─────────────────┐
│                 │
│  Photograph of  │
│    Narrator     │
│                 │
└─────────────────┘
```

Project name:	
For further information and a project brief, please contact:	
Interview length	
Archival/unedited	
Edited	
Interview number	
Name of narrator	
Language of interview	
Narrator languages	
Interpreter details if used	
Narrator address	
Narrator telephone/e-mail	
Date and place of birth	
Date of Interview	
Place of Interview	
Name of Interviewer	
Interviewer address	
Interviewer telephone/e-mail	

Technical Data – Sound Files

Brand and Model of Digital Recorder	
Brand and microphones type	
Sound Storage	
Back-up location	
Digital Recording Rate	
Sound Field	
Audio editing program	
Audio editing methodology	

Technical Data – Photographs/Images

Images provided by narrator	
Photograph(s) owner/creator	
Source Access/Restrictions/Copyright	
Model of Digital Camera	
File Format (e.g. JPG)	
Pixel dimension	

Documentation

Signed Release Form?	
Transcript completed? Summary?	
List of other relevant documentation	

Field Notes

Timed Annotated Log

Time	Content	Details Names in first name, family name format	Post recorded information and confirmation sessions
0:00-	Project introduction		

Source: Ideas presented in this chart are based on Oral History NSW. 2014. "Useful templates for Oral History documentation." Oral History NSW www.oralhistorynsw.org.au/useful-templates-for-oral-history-documentation.html. Accessed February 15, 2015.

Appendix C: Generic Introduction and Initial Interview Questions

This is <u>name of interviewer</u> interviewing <u>name of narrator</u> on <u>date</u> at <u>specific location</u> <u>details</u> for <u>name of oral history project</u>. (<u>Name of interpreter and details</u> [if used]).

Sample introductory questions:
Please tell me your full name and spell it please.
When and where were you born?
What were your parent's names?
Where was your mother born and when?
Where was your father born and when?
Do you know any details about your grandparents?
What was your mother's occupation?
What was your father's occupation?
Please give the names of your brothers and sisters.
Please give the names of your children.

INTERVIEW

Concluding question: Is there anything more you would like to add?

Thanks given
This is the conclusion of interview number _____ for the name of project. This is interview number _____ with name of narrator.

Appendix D: Trauma Support Services

STARTTS is the NSW Service for the Treatment and Rehabilitation of Torture and Trauma Survivors. STARTTS provides services to assist people from refugee and refugee-like backgrounds who have experienced torture or other traumatic events before arriving in Australia. They help individual refugees and families recover from their experiences, work with refugee community groups to foster empowerment and self-determination, and support other organisations and individuals working with refugees. STARTTS is one of Australia's leading organisations for the treatment and rehabilitation of torture and trauma survivors. www.startts.org.au/

beyondblue is an independent, not-for-profit organisation working to increase awareness and understanding of anxiety and depression in Australia and to reduce the associated stigma. beyondblue is a bipartisan initiative of the Australian Federal, State, and Territory Governments supported by the generosity of individuals, fund-raising initiatives, and corporate Australia. beyondblue has partnered with Mental Health in Multicultural Australia (MHiMA) to work with key organisations, refugees, and migrants to reduce the impact of depression and anxiety among culturally and linguistically diverse communities. beyondblue has also translated resources into over twenty-five languages. www.beyondblue.org.au/

Lifeline is a national charity providing Australians experiencing a personal crisis with access to twenty-four-hour crisis support and suicide prevention services. Lifeline's twenty-four-hour crisis line helps people with: suicidal thoughts or attempts; personal crisis; anxiety; depression; loneliness; abuse and trauma; stresses from work, family, or society; and self-help information for friends and family. Lifeline is a national charity and relies on community support. www.lifeline.org.au/

TAFE NSW Careers and Counselling Services—among other roles TAFE Counsellors help students with personal matters such as: anxiety and depression, health, relationships, and drug and alcohol problems. They also organise referrals to appropriate services. Personal counselling services are provided on a one-to-one, confidential basis at TAFE NSW campuses. Some campuses offer both day and evening services, or offer bilingual counsellors who can give assistance in a first language. www.tafensw.edu.au/services/counselling/#.VM0wojp03IU

Appendix E: Networking: Organizations & Professional Associations

The best way to keep up with current information in a rapidly evolving field is to go straight to the source. These organizations and online discussion groups will keep you up to date with workshops, publications, discussion, and practical tips.

American Association of State and Local History (AASLH)
- Conference • Publications • Professional standards (Statement of Professional Standards and Ethics, 2002) • Workshops • Assessment tools

American Historical Association (AHA)
- Conference • Career center and professional development • Publications: *American Historical Review*, publication series • Professional standards (Statement on Standards of Professional Conduct, 2005)

Association for Recorded Sound Collections (ARSC)
- Conference • Online discussion group • Publications: *ARSC Journal, ARSC Newsletter, ARSC Bulletin* • Grants and awards

The Association of Moving Image Archivists (AMIA)
- Conference • Online discussion group • Publications: *The Moving Image, AMIA Newsletter* • Online Resources • Scholarships and awards • Professional standards (Code of Ethics)

Association of Personal Historians (APH)
- Conference • Online Resources • Regional chapters • Professional standards (Code of Ethics) • Educational programs

Australian Centre for the Moving Image (ACMI)
- Digital Storytelling training

Australian Copyright Council
- Seminars • Legal Advice • User-friendly information sheets

Baylor University Institute for Oral History (BUIOH)
- Workshops • Online Resources • Fellowships • Training manuals

Center for Digital Storytelling, Berkeley, California
- Online Resources • Workshops & Tutorials

Creative Commons (CC). Nonprofit organization offering a flexible copyright option for creative work. This is an option that lies between full copyright and public domain.
- Online discussion group • Online Resources • Creative Commons decision tree

H-NET (Humanities and Social Sciences Online). Network of scholars and teachers who use the web to distribute information to a wide audience.
- Online discussion groups: supports a large number of moderated discussion groups in particular topics in the sciences and humanities, including H-ORALHIST (oral history), H-MUSEUM (museum studies) and H-PUBLIC (public history) • Publications: online book reviews.

Image Permanence Institute. Hosted by College of Imaging Arts and Sciences, Rochester Institute of Technology. Devoted to scientific research in the preservation of recorded information.
- Publications • Workshops • Online resources

Independent Media Arts Preservation (IMAP). Non-profit service, education, and advocacy organization committed to the preservation of non-commercial electronic media.
- Online Resources • Workshops & tutorials • Cataloging tutorial and template for media collections

International Association of Sound and Audiovisual Archives (IASA)
- Conference • Publications: *IASA Journal*, guidelines and best practices for cataloging sound recordings, preservation of digital audio and others • Online Resources • Professional standards

International Oral History Association (IOHA)
- Conference • Online discussion group • Publications • Blog

Library of Congress. U.S. national library website serves as a portal for the library's catalog, American Memory Project, Veterans Oral History Project, National Recording Preservation Board, and information on digital preservation.
   • Publications • Online Resources • Workshops & Tutorials • Professional standards

MATRIX, Center for Digital Humanities and Social Sciences, Michigan State University. This center supports the use of digital technology for projects in the humanities and social sciences. Platform for Historical Voices and Oral History in the Digital Age.
   • Online Resources • Best practices • Project support

National Council on Public History (NCPH)
   • Conference • Awards • Learning tools • Publications: *Public Historian, Public History News*, and other pamphlets and videos

National Library of Australia
   • Oral history and Folklore collection • Online listening collection

Oral History Association (OHA). United States' professional association for oral historians.
   • Conference • Publications: *Oral History Review, OHA Newsletter*, pamphlet series, blog • Online Resources • Professional standards: Evaluation guidelines, Rev. 2000

Oral History Society. United Kingdom's professional association for oral historians.
   • Conference • Publications • Online Resources • Career center

Oral History Australia. Australia's professional association for oral historians.
   • Conference • Publications • Online Resources • Training • State-based oral history associations

Professional Historians Australia (PHA)
   • Conference • Newsletter • Resources • State and Territory Professional Historian Associations

United States Copyright Office. Administers the registration and regulation of copyright in the United States.
   • Publications • Online Resources

NOTES

Notes to Preface

1. Australian Bureau of Statistics. 2012–2013. "Cultural Diversity in Australia Reflecting a Nation: Stories from the 2011 Census." ABS. Accessed February 15, 2015. www.abs.gov.au/ausstats/abs@.nsf/Lookup/2071.0main+featur es902012-2013.

Notes to Chapter 1

1. Green, Anna. 2008. "Oral History Interview." *The TAFE NSW Sutherland College Oral History Project*, October 17, 2008. Accessed February 15, 2015. http://oralhistory.sydneyinstitute.wikispaces.net/Anna+Green.
2. Ibid.
3. Kuiper, Tina. 2008. "Oral History Interview." *The TAFE NSW Sutherland College Oral History Project*, October 31, 2008. Accessed February 15, 2015. http://oralhistory.sydneyinstitute.wikispaces.net/Tina+Kuiper.
4. Kamich, Rachael. 2011. "Oral History Interview." *Sudanese People in the Sutherland Shire – A Moving Community Oral History Project*. Accessed February 15, 2015. http://oralhistory.sydneyinstitute.wikispaces.net/Sudanese+people+in+th e+Sutherland+Shire+-+a+moving+community%2C+oral+history+project.
5. "The Snowy Mountains Scheme." 2008. australia.gov.au. Accessed February 15, 2015. http://australia.gov.au/about-australia/australian-story/snowy-mountains-scheme.
6. "The Six O'Clock Swill." 1999. Dinkum Aussies. Accessed February 15, 2015. www.dinkumaussies.com/EVENTS%2FThe%20Six%20O%27clock%20 Swill.htm.
7. DeAngelis, Luigi. 2008/2009. "Oral History Interviews." *The TAFE NSW Sutherland College Oral History Project*, October 10, 2008, April 3, 2009. Accessed February 15, 2015. http://oralhistory.sydneyinstitute.wikispaces.net/Luigi+DeAngelis.
8. Van Der Sloot, Rosalin. 2008/2009. "Oral History Interviews." *The TAFE NSW Sutherland College Oral History Project*, October 29, 2008, September 9, 2009.

Accessed February 15, 2015. http://oralhistory.sydneyinstitute.wikispaces.net/Rose+Van+Der+Sloot.

9. Magnus, Bob. 2008. "Oral History Interview." *The TAFE NSW Sutherland College Oral History Project*, June 8, 2008. Accessed February 15, 2015. http://oralhistory.sydneyinstitute.wikispaces.net/Bob+Magnus.

10. "Guidelines of Ethical Practice." 2015. Oral History Australia. Accessed February 15, 2015. www.oralhistoryaustralia.org.au/page/guidelines_of_ethical_practice.html. "Principles and Best Practices." 2009. Oral History Association USA. October 2009. Accessed February 15, 2015. www.oralhistory.org/about/principles-and-practices/.

11. "Introduction to the Dreaming." 2015. Indigenous Australia. Accessed February 15, 2015. www.indigenousaustralia.info/the-dreaming.html.

12. "Oral Traditions." 2015. Indigenous Australia. Accessed February 15, 2015. www.indigenousaustralia.info/languages/oral-traditions.html.

13. "Oral Traditions." 2009. Indigenous Foundations. Accessed February 15, 2015. http://indigenousfoundations.arts.ubc.ca/home/culture/oral-traditions.html.

14. "Literacy Rate, Adult Total (% of People Ages 15 and above)." 2015. The World Bank. Accessed February 15, 2015. http://data.worldbank.org/indicator/SE.ADT.LITR.ZS.

15. "World Migration in Figures." 2013. OECD-UNDESA, Oct. 2013. Accessed February 15, 2015. www.oecd.org/els/mig/World-Migration-in-Figures.pdf.

16. Everett, Lee. 1966. "A Theory of Migration." *Demography* 3 (1): 47–57.

17. Australian Bureau of Statistics; United States Census. "IT'S IN OUR HANDS." 2010. Accessed February 15, 2015. www.census.gov/2010census/.

18. Frerichs, Sandra, and Lesley Quinn. 2012. *Australian Migration (1945 Onwards) Post WWII*. Bendigo: VEA Group Pty Ltd.

19. Markus, Andrew, James Jupp, and Peter McDonald. 2009. *Australia's Immigration Revolution*. Crows Nest: Allen & Unwin.

Notes to Chapter 2

1. Sutherland Shire Council. 2011. "Oral History Interview." *Sudanese People in the Sutherland Shire – a Moving Community Oral History Project*. Accessed February 15, 2015. http://oralhistory.sydneyinstitute.wikispaces.net/Sudanese+people+in+the+Sutherland+Shire+-+a+moving+community%2C+oral+history+project.

2. NSW Migration Heritage Centre. 2010. "Frequently Asked Questions." Accessed February 15, 2015. www.migrationheritage.nsw.gov.au/about-us/frequently-asked-questions/.

3. Thompson, Paul. 2000. *Voice of the Past: Oral History*. Oxford: Oxford University Press.

4. Browne, Peter. 2006. *The Longest Journey: Resettling Refugees from Africa*. Sydney: University of New South Wales Press.

5. Names withheld. 2011. "Oral History Vox Pop Interviews." *Sudanese People in the Sutherland Shire – a Moving Community Oral History Project.* Accessed February 15, 2015. http://oralhistory.sydneyinstitute.wikispaces.net/Sudanese+people+in+t he+Sutherland+Shire+-+a+moving+community%2C+oral+history+project.

6. "Vox Pops." 2015. Media College. Accessed February 15, 2015. www.mediacollege. com/video/interviews/voxpops.html.

7. "Life in Southern Sudan." 2011. NSW Migration Heritage Centre. Accessed February 15, 2015. www.migrationheritage.nsw.gov.au/exhibition/sudanesestories/ life-in-southern-sudan/.

8. "A Brief History of Romanian Immigration to Minnesota." 2014. Heritage Organization of Romanian Americans in Minnesota. Accessed February 15, 2015. www.hora-mn.org/.

9. "News." 2014. Heritage Organization of Romanian Americans in Minnesota. Accessed February 15, 2015. www.hora-mn.org/news.html.

10. Janiszewski, Leonard, and Effy Alexakis. 2005. "In Their Own Image: Greek-Australians National Project Past, Present, and Potential Future." In *Greek Research in Australia: Proceedings of the Sixth Biennial International Conference of Greek Studies*, edited by E. Close, M. Tsianikas, and G. Couvalis, 123–134. Melbourne: Flinders University.

11. Ibid.

12. "Selling an American Dream: Australia's Greek Café." National Museum of Australia. Accessed February 15, 2015. www.nma.gov.au/exhibitions/selling_ an_american_dream_australias_greek_cafe/home.

13. Janiszewski, Leonard and Effy Alexakis. 2012. "Telling Tales of Australia's Country Greek Cafés: A Project Insight." *Communities of Memory/Oral History Association Australia* 34: 3–13.

14. "Oakland Chinatown Oral History Project." 2014. Oakland Asian Cultural Center. Accessed February 15, 2015. http://oacc.cc/oakland-chinatown-oral-history-project/.

15. Ma, L. Eve Armentrout. 2000. *Hometown Chinatown: The History of Oakland's Chinese Community.* New York: Garland Publishing.

16. Phillips, Denise. 2010. "Hazaras' Persecution Worsens: Will the New Government Show Leadership by Lifting the Suspension on Afghani Asylum Claims?" *Australian Policy and History*, Aug. 2010. Accessed February 15, 2015. http://e-publications.une.edu.au/1959.11/7267.

17. "Hazara People." 2015. Wikipedia. Accessed February 15, 2015. http:// en.wikipedia.org/wiki/Hazara_people. Phillips, Denise. 2011. "Wounded Memory of Hazara Refugees: Remembering and Forgetting Persecution." *History Australia* 8 (2): 178.

18. SBS staff. 2013. "Explainer: Who Are the Hazaras?" SBS News. September 2013. Accessed February 15, 2015. www.sbs.com.au/news/article/2013/03/20/ explainer-who-are-hazaras.

19. Ibid.

20. Phillips, Denise. 2014. "From Afghanistan to Australia: An Oral History Study of the Experiences of Loss and Hope among Hazara Refugees: Working Summary from Unpublished Forthcoming PhD Thesis." University of New England.

21. Phillips, Denise. 2005. "'I'm 21 and Have No Any Happy Days': An Oral History Narrative from the Hazara Refugee Community." *Oral History Association of Australia Journal* 27:28–33.

22. Phillips, Denise. 2014. "'To Dream My Family Tonight': Listening to Stories of Grief and Hope among Hazara Refugees in Australia." In *Listening on the Edge: Oral History in the Aftermath of Crisis*, edited by Mark Cave and Stephen Sloan, 33-54. New York: Oxford University Press.

23. Phillips Denise. 2010. "Hazaras' Persecution Worsens: Will the New Government Show Leadership by Lifting the Suspension on Afghani Asylum Claims?" Australian Policy and History, Aug. 2010. Accessed February 15, 2015 http://e-publications.une.edu.au/1959.11/7267.

Notes to Chapter 3

1. Fifer, Stephen. 2011. "Oral History Interview." *Sudanese People in the Sutherland Shire – A Moving Community Oral History Project.* Accessed February 15, 2015. http://oralhistory.sydneyinstitute.wikispaces.net/Sudanese+people+in+the+Sutherland+Shire+-+a+moving+community%2C+oral+history+project.

2. Robinson, Lawrence, Melinda Smith, Jeanne Segal. 2015. "Emotional and Psychological Trauma." HelpGuide. February, 2015. Accessed February 15, 2015. www.helpguide.org/mental/emotional_psychological_trauma.htm.

3. Australian Centre for Posttraumatic Mental Health. 2013. "Trauma and Mental Health." *The Australian Guidelines for the Treatment of ASD and PTSD*, September, 2013. Accessed February 15, 2015. www.acpmh.unimelb.edu.au/trauma/impact_of_trauma.html?_ga=1.243142914.1036136642.1424988358.

4. "Trauma." 2015. American Psychological Association. Accessed February 15, 2015. www.apa.org/topics/trauma/.

5. Australian Centre for Posttraumatic Mental Health. 2013. "What Is Trauma?" Accessed February 15, 2015. www.acpmh.unimelb.edu.au/search.html?q=what+is+trauma.

6. American Psychiatric Association. 2000. *The Diagnostic and Statistical Manual of Mental Disorders*, 4th edition. Accessed February 15, 2015. www.sagepub.com/upm-data/11559_Chapter_1.pdf.

7. Doran, Gaye. 2011. "Oral History Interview." *Sudanese People in the Sutherland Shire – a Moving Community Oral History Project.* Accessed February 15, 2015. http://oralhistory.sydneyinstitute.wikispaces.net/Sudanese+people+in+the+Sutherland+Shire+-+a+moving+community%2C+oral+history+project.

8. Nadel, Lynne and W. Jake Jacobs. 1998. "Traumatic Memory Is Special." American Psychological Society. Accessed February 15, 2015. www.u.arizona. edu/~nadel/pdf/Papers%20as%20PDFs/1998%20PDFs/Current%20Directions%2098.pdf.

9. Morris, Ben. 2014. "The Diggers' Wish: Set the Record Straight." *'She Said: He Said:' Reading, Writing and Recording History Oral History Australia Journal* 36: 72–85.

10. See Support Services Appendix.

11. See Support Services Appendix.

12. "Post-traumatic stress disorder." 2015. beyondblue. Accessed February 15, 2015. www.beyondblue.org.au/.

13. Kelham, Megg. 2012. "Creating and Confronting Community: Suicide Stories in Central Australia." *Communities of Memory Oral History Australia* 34: 54–61.

14. Phillips, Denise. 2011. "Wounded Memory of Hazara Refugees: Remembering and Forgetting Persecution." *History Australia* 8 (2): 177–198.

15. Churchill, Winston. 2015. "Miscellaneous Wit & Wisdom Quotes." National Churchill Museum. Accessed February 15, 2015. www.nationalchurchillmuseum. org/wit-wisdom-quotes.html.

16. Kamich, Rachael. 2011. "Oral History Interview."

17. Leith, Denise. 2013. "The Garden." In *A Country Too Far: Writings on Asylum Seekers*, edited by Rosie Scott and Tom Keneally, 85. Australia: Penguin.

18. Gadi, BenEzer. 2004. "Trauma Signals in Life Stories." In *Trauma: Life Stories of Survivors*, edited by Kim Lacy Rogers, Selma Leydesdorff, and Graham Dawson, 29–44. New Brunswick: Transaction Publishers.

19. Hin, Savan. 2014. "Oral History Interview." March 28, 2014. Accessed February 15, 2015. www.historyherstory.com.au/products--services.html.

20. De Nike, Howard J. 2000. "Reflections of a Legal Anthropologist on the Trial of Pol Pot and Leng Sary." In *Genocide in Cambodia: Documents from the Trial of Pol Pot and Leng Sary*, edited by Howard J. De Nike, John Quigley, and Kenneth Robinson, 19–28. Philadelphia: University of Pennsylvania Press.

21. Morris, "The Diggers' Wish.

22. BenEzer. "Trauma Signals in Life Stories."

23. Klempner, Mark. 2010. "Navigating Life Review Interviews with Survivors of Trauma." In *The Oral History Reader,* edited by Robert Perks and Alistair Thomson, 198–210. USA and Canada: Routledge.

24. Green, Anna. 2008. "Oral History Interview."

25. Nguyen, Huyen. 2008/2009. "Oral History Interviews." *The TAFE NSW Sutherland College Oral History Project*, October 23, 2008, May 5, 2009. Accessed February 15, 2015.

26. Van Der Sloot, Rosalin. 2008/2009. "Oral History Interviews."

27. Des Pres, Terrence. 1991. *Writing into the World. Essays: 1973–1987.* New York: Viking.
28. Phillips, Denise. 2011. "Report: Making Memories and Meaning from the 16th IOHA Conference in Prague." *Communities of Memory Oral History Australia* 33: 63–68.
29. Greenspan, Henry. 2010. *On Listening to Holocaust Survivors: Beyond Testimony.* St. Paul, MN: Paragon House.
30. Yousif, Anwar. 2008. "Oral History Interview." *The TAFE NSW Sutherland College Oral History Project*, October 24, 2008. Accessed February 15, 2015. http://oralhistory.sydneyinstitute.wikispaces.net/Anwar+Yousif.
31. Des Pres, Terrence. 1988. "Holocaust Laughter?" In *Writing and the Holocaust*, edited by Berel Lang, 216–233. New York: Holmes & Meier.
32. Vital Hearts. 2013. "Secondary Trauma." The Resiliency Training Initiative. www.vitalhearts.org/.
33. Ibid.
34. Bicknell-Hentges, Lindsay, and John J. Lynch. 2009. "Everything Counselors and Supervisors Need to Know About Treating Trauma." Paper based on a presentation at the American Counseling Association Annual Conference and Exposition, Charlotte, NC, March, 2009.

Notes to Chapter 4

1. DeAngelis, Luigi. 2008/2009. "Oral History Interviews." (NB. In NSW, Australia, a schooner of beer is 425 millilitres or 15 fluid ounces).
2. Messner, Wolfgang. 2013. *Intercultural Communication Competence.* Bangalore: GloBus Research.
3. O'Sullivan, Kerry. 1994. *Understanding Ways, Communicating between Cultures.* Sydney: Hale and Iremonger.
4. Messner, *Intercultural Communication Competence*, p. 16.
5. Harman, Hakan. 2014. "Multicultural News." NSW Government, October 29, 2014. Accessed February 15, 2015. www.crc.nsw.gov.au/about_crc/media_releases/latest_media_releases/documents2/2014/speak_out.
6. Australian Bureau of Statistics. www.abs.gov.au/.
7. Humes, Karen, R. Jones, Nicholas A., and Roberto R. Ramirez. 2011. "Overview of Race and Hispanic Origin: 2010." 2010 Census Briefs, March, 2011. Accessed February 15, 2015. www.census.gov/prod/cen2010/briefs/c2010br-02.pdf.
8. United States Census, 2010.
9. "Terminology." 2015. NSW Government. Accessed February 15, 2015. www.crc.nsw.gov.au/mpsp/terminology.
10. Cotton, Gayle. 2013. *Say Anything to Anyone, Anywhere: 5 Keys to Successful Cross-Cultural Communication.* New Jersey: John Wiley & Sons.

11. Storti, Craig. 1999. *Figuring Foreigners Out: A Practical Guide.* Boston: Intercultural Press.

12. Baxamusa, Batul Nafisa. 2010. "Hand Gestures in Different Cultures." Buzzle, May 19, 2010. Accessed February 15, 2015. www.buzzle.com/articles/hand-gestures-in-different-cultures.html.

13. Axtell, Roger E. 1998. *Gestures: The DOs and TABOOS of Body Language around the World.* New York: John Wiley & Sons, p. 38.

14. Ibid, pp. 67–69.

Notes to Chapter 6

1. "Consecutive Interpreting." 2015. DC Spanish Interpreting Breaking the Language Barrier. Accessed February 15, 2015. www.dcspanish.com/pages/4/.

2. McLean, Philippa, Kate Perkins, Dave Tout, Kath Brewer, and Linda Wyse. 2012. *Australian Core Skills Framework.* Canberra: Department of Industry, Innovation, Science, Research and Tertiary Education.

3. "TOEFL." 2015. *ETS.* Accessed February 15, 2015. www.ets.org/toefl?WT. ac=toeflhome_why_121127.

4. "Guide for Agents." 2015. IELTS. Accessed February 15, 2015. www.ielts.org/ pdf/IELTS%20Guide%20for%20Agents_web_2013.pdf+.

5. McLean et al. Ibid.

6. "List of Languages by Number of Native Speakers in India." 2015. Wikipedia. Accessed February 15, 2015. http://en.wikipedia.org/wiki/List_of_ languages_by_number_of_native_speakers_in_India.

7. "Languages of China." 2015. Wikipedia. Accessed February 15, 2015. http:/ en.wikipedia.org/wiki/Languages_of_China. "Languages of Africa." 2015.Wikipedia. Accessed February 15, 2015. http://en.wikipedia.org/wiki/Languages_ of_Africa.

8. "Languages of Africa." 2015. Wikipedia. Accessed February 15, 2015. http:// en.wikipedia.org/wiki/Languages_of_Africa.

Notes to Chapter 7

1. Doran, Gaye. 2011. "Oral History Interview

2. Yousif, Anwar. 2008. "Oral History Interview."

3. Hin, Savan. 2014. "Oral History Interview."

4. Doran, Gaye. 2011. "Oral History Interview."

5. Green, Anna. 2008. "Oral History Interview."

6. "Pict-Oral Memoir." 2015. Legacy Stories.org. Your stories making history. Accessed February 15, 2015. www.legacystories.org/about/legacy-matters-family.

7. "Digital Photo Stories." 2015. History Herstory: RETELL RECORD RETAIN. Accessed February 15, 2015. www.historyherstory.com.au/products--services.html.
8. "Create your first photo story." 2015. Windows. Accessed February 15, 2015. http://windows.microsoft.com/en-US/windows-xp/help/digitalphotography/create-first-photo-story.

Notes to Chapter 8

1. "Guidelines of Ethical Practice." Oral History Australia. www.oralhistoryaustralia.org.au/ "Principles and Best Practices." Oral History Association USA. http://www.oralhistory.org/.
2. See Appendices.
3. "Oral History Association Response to Developments in Boston College Case." 2015. Oral History Association USA. Accessed February 15, 2015. www.oralhistory.org/2014/05/05/oral-history-association-response-to-developments-in-boston-college-case/.
4. "Working With Children Check." 2015. NSW Government, Accessed February 15, 2015. www.kidsguardian.nsw.gov.au/working-with-children/working-with-children-check.
5. See Appendices.

Notes to Chapter 9

1. Hin, Savan. 2014. "Oral History Interview."
2. Schanberg, Sydney. 2011. "Cambodia." Crimes of War. Accessed February 15, 2015. www.crimesofwar.org/a-z-guide/cambodia/.
3. Ponchaud, Francois. 1978. *Cambodia Year Zero.* New York: Holt, Rinehart and Winston.
4. Hin, Savan. 2014. "Oral History Interview."
5. Ibid.
6. Ponchaud, *Cambodia Year Zero.*
7. Kamm, Henry. 1998. *Cambodia: Report from a Stricken Land.* New York: Arcade Publishing.
8. Schanberg, 2011. "Cambodia." Crimes of War.
9. Bergin, Sean. 2009. *The Khmer Rouge and the Cambodian Genocide.* New York: The Rosen Publishing Group.
10. Hin, Savan. 2014. "Oral History Interview."

GLOSSARY

Analog (also spelled analogue). A process that records and stores information such as sound or images in a continuous pattern.

Archives. The agency responsible for selecting, acquiring, preserving, and making available archival materials.

Asylum Seeker. A person who crosses an international border into a country in which he or she hopes to be granted refugee status and international protection.

Bit rate. The number of bits processed in a given unit of time.

Born digital. A document created in a digital format, such as a text document created through word processing, or an interview recorded on a digital recorder.

CD (Compact disc). An optical medium for recording and storing data.

Collection. A group of documents that are related in some way, such as the papers of a person, or an oral history series. The collection should be identified as a unit with a name and title associated with it.

Community. Any group with a shared identity.

Contract. A legally binding agreement involving two or more parties, requiring some kind of consideration (payment) and specifying what each party will or will not do.

Copying. An important preservation principle referring to reproducing the content of a resource. Copies can be made from one format to another, one medium to another, or to an exact representation of the original.

Copyright. The exclusive right reproduce, publish, or sell copies of original creations (such as oral history interviews), and to license their production and sale by others. Copyright is granted by the U.S. federal government for a specified period of time. National copyright laws vary but have the same fundamental understandings.

Cultural heritage. The history, beliefs, stories, ceremonies, law, language, symbols, land, and artefacts that are shared by a group of people and that make up their culture.

Curation. The practice of long-term management and care of historical documents and artefacts, in order to ensure maximum access into the indefinite future.

Data compression. Digital information that is copied to a representation using fewer bits than the original. Data compression results in smaller digital files and sometimes a loss in quality.

Deed of gift. A signed, written agreement which transfers ownership without monetary consideration. Most oral histories are passed from the interviewer or narrator to the archive through a deed of gift.

Defamation. A false statement of fact printed or broadcast about a person, which tends to injure that person's interest.

Digital. A process that captures and stores information in discrete values, usually measured in bits (zeroes or ones) and bytes.

Digital storytelling. A popular method for recording and preserving personal or family stories using multimedia.

Digitization. The act of transferring a sound recording from analog (continuous wave) format to digital (samples of the sound wave converted to bits and bytes).

Document. A generic term to describe a unit of information in the physical or the virtual world. A document can be a book, a broadside, or an oral history transcript or recording in the physical world.

DVD. Originally Digital Video Disc, then Digital Versatile Disc, currently doesn't stand for anything at all. An optical disc used for storing digital information. DVDs hold much more information than CDs but less is known about their preservation qualities.

Emigrant. Someone who leaves their home country or region to settle elsewhere.

ESB. English Speaking Background describes people and communities who speak English as their first language. ·

Fair use. A provision in copyright law that allows the limited use of copyrighted materials for teaching, research, scholarship, or news reporting purposes.

File. A unit defining related data in a computerized environment, often referred to as a document. A file can be a text document, a spreadsheet, an image, or an audio file.

Gift. Voluntary transfer of property without getting anything in return. Oral histories are generally transferred to repositories as gifts.

Historical record. Any document or artefact that is historically significant and is available to the public in an archive, library, government office, or digital repository.

Immigrant. Someone who moves, for numerous reasons, to live in another country, usually permanently. Immigrants are also known as migrants.

Informed consent. An agreement to do something or allow something to happen, made with complete knowledge of all relevant facts, such as the risks involved or any available alternatives. In oral history, the interviewer's job is to provide informed consent to the narrator about the intended use of the interview.

Intellectual property. The area of law that regulates the ownership and use of creative works, including patent, copyright, and trademark.

Interview. A structured question and answer session between a narrator and interviewer characterised by well-focussed, clearly stated, open-ended, neutral questions aimed at gathering information not available from other sources. The interview is the basis for all oral history.

Interviewee. Interviewee is synonymous with narrator.

Interviewer. The person who asks questions and guides the structure of an interview.

Legal release agreement. The signed, legal agreement between the interviewee and the interviewer that clarifies conditions for the interview, such as intent (reasons for conducting the interview), delivery and acceptance (of the interview itself to the designated party), copyright assignment (usually turned over to the interviewer or repository), and narrator's rights to future use.

L1. First Language.

L2. Second Language.

Life interview. An oral history interview that focusses on the life of one person, usually in a series of interviews. Many oral histories are a combination of life and topical interviews.

Local history. The study of history in a geographically specific context that often concentrates on the local community.

LOCKSS (Lots of Copies Keeps Stuff Safe). A simple preservation principle referring to the benefits of making multiple copies in multiple formats and storing in multiple locations, as a means to preserve the content if one copy is destroyed.

Memory. The ability of a human being to perceive, process, and recall information. Oral history is a methodology of recounting of individuals' memories.

Microhistory. The intensive historical investigation of a well-defined smaller unit of research (most often a single event, a village, a family, or a person). Microhistory can be distinguished from a case study insofar as it concentrates on asking big questions as they relate to small research topics.

Microphone. A device that converts sound to electrical signals, usually for amplification. Microphones exist inside recorders as well as separate devices.

Migrant. Someone who moves, for numerous reasons, to live in another country, usually permanently. Migrants are also known as immigrants.

Narrator. The person being interviewed, also known as the interviewee.

NESB. Non-English Speaking Background describes people and communities whose first language is a language other than English.

Open source. Computer application in which the source code is openly available. Open source applications are usually developed collaboratively.

Optical media. Media, such as CDs and DVDs, that use laser technology for data storage and retrieval.

Oral history. 1. The documentation of recent history by means of a recorded, structured interview. 2. The discipline that has grown up around this methodology. 3. A "package" which includes an interview or series of interviews related by content, often with transcript and supporting materials, made available for public use.

Oral tradition. A community's cultural and historical background preserved and passed on from one generation to the next in spoken stories and song, as distinct from a written tradition.

Ownership. The person or legal entity that holds physical posession of the item, along with all the accompanying rights and responsibilities.

Primary source. Firsthand information with no interpretation between the document and the researcher. An oral history is a primary resource, as are diaries and correspondence.

Processing. The organization, description, and arrangement of documents to make them available for public use.

Project. A series of tasks to accomplish a specific outcome within a specific time period. In the case of oral history, a number of interviews around a particular topic or for a particular purpose.

Public domain. A creative work that is not subject to the copyright laws and may be used without permission of the creator or former rights holder. The work could either be expressly created for the public domain or have an expired copyright limitation.

Public history. History that is seen, read, heard, or interpreted by a popular audience.

Public record. The full body of information available to the public through libraries, historical societies, government agencies, and the Internet. Information can include all books, journals, laws, and government documents. It contrasts to the information which has restricted access for any reason.

Record. 1. Any document which supports a function, such as "keeping records on the project." 2. A document created or received by an agency, organization, or individual, in pursuance of legal obligations or business transactions. 3. An element in the hierarchical structure of a database. A record contains related fields, and is contained in a file.

Refugee. A person who flees their country to a foreign country for protection or safety.

Repository. A physical space with a long-term preservation plan for materials that go into the historical record. Libraries, archives, historical societies, museums, and digital repositories are examples of repositories. *See also* **archives.**

Restriction. Limitation imposed (usually) by the narrator to legally restrict access to all or part of the interview content, for a limited time or permanently.

Sampling rate. The number of samples from a sound wave that the computer takes to make a digital file. The larger the sample the higher the quality of sound and the closest the digital sound represents the original.

Secondary source. Interpretations of history based on the evidence contained in primary sources. Secondary sources involve generalization, analysis, synthesis, interpretation, or evaluation of the original information. Primary and secondary are relative terms, and some sources may be classified as primary or secondary, depending on how they are used.

Shared authority. A best practice in oral history which recognizes the contributions of both the narrator and the interviewer in the interview process.

Slander. Spoken statement that can damage another person's reputation.

Summary. A condensation of an interview, highlighting the key points. A summary can be a paragraph to a few pages long, depending on the purpose. Summaries are useful for curators evaluating a collection, for catalogers, for researchers, and for websites or printed catalogs.

Timed index. An annotated list of topics covered in the interview, indexed at timed intervals. A timed index is a useful tool for researchers to find sections on an audiotape, but is less useful if the sound is edited, rearranged, or transferred to another medium.

Topical interview. An oral history interview based on a particular topic, event, or community.

Transcript. A verbatim version of the spoken word. A transcript matches the interview as closely as possible and contains the full and accurately spelled names of all persons and places mentioned in the interview.

Video. A method of capturing, recording, processing, transmitting, and re-constructing moving images using film, electronic signals, or digital media.

Visual history. A recorded oral history interview using video instead of audio.

Further Reading

Doing Oral History

Boyd, Douglas A. and Mary A. Larson, eds. 2014. *Oral History and Digital Humanities: Voice, Access, and Engagement*. New York: Palgrave Macmillan.

Charlton, Thomas L., Lois E. Myers, and M. Rebecca Sharpless, eds. 2006. *Handbook of Oral History*. Walnut Creek, CA: AltaMira Press.

Dudding, Michael. 2008. *Abstracting Oral Histories (A How-To Guide)*. Wellington, NZ: Victoria University of Wellington.

Frisch, Michael. 1990. *A Shared Authority: Essays on the Craft and Meaning of Oral and Public History*. Albany: State University of New York Press.

Gwinn-Becker, Kristen. 2014. The Future of History (video). Portland, ME: TedX Dirigo. www.youtube.com/watch?v=Vju9fnOwMts.

H-ORALHIST (Online community). Moderated H-Net discussion group serves the oral history community. Subscription information and archives at https://networks.h-net.org/h-oralhist.

Hamilton, Paula and Linda Shopes, eds. 2008. *Oral History and Public Memories*. Philadelphia, PA: Temple University Press.

Mackay, Nancy, Barbara W. Sommer, and Mary Kay Quinlan. 2013. *Community Oral History Toolkit*. 5 vols. Walnut Creek, CA: Left Coast Press. See especially v.5. *After the Interview in Community Oral History*.

Perks, Robert, and Alistair Thomson, eds. 2006. *The Oral History Reader*. 2nd ed. London: Routledge.

Ritchie, Donald A. 2015. *Doing Oral History*. 3rd ed. Oxford: Oxford University Press.

Robertson, Beth M. 2006. *Oral History Handbook*. 5th ed. South Australia: Oral History Association of Australia (South Australian Branch).

Schneider, William, ed. 2008. *Living with Stories: Telling, Re-telling, and Remembering*. Logan: Utah State University Press.

Shopes, Linda. 2012. "Transcribing Oral History in the Digital Age." In *Oral History in the Digital Age*, edited by Doug Boyd, Steve Cohen, Brad Rakerd, and Dean Rehberger. Washington, DC: Institute of Museum and Library Services. http://ohda.matrix.msu.edu/2012/06/transcribing-oral-history-in-the-digital-age/.

Sommer, Barbara W. and Mary Kay Quinlan. 2009. *The Oral History Manual*. 2nd ed. Lanham, MD: AltaMira Press.

Thompson, Paul. 2000. *The Voice of the Past: Oral History*. 3rd ed. Oxford: Oxford University Press.

Trower, Shelley, ed. 2011. *Place, Writing, and Voice in Oral History.* New York: Palgrave Macmillan.

Web Guides to Doing Oral History. 2015. Oral History Association. Accessed January 31, 2015. Frequently updated list of links to oral history project manuals. www.oralhistory.org/web-guides-to-doing-oral-history/.

Zusman, Angela. 2010. *Story Bridges: A Guide for Conducting Intergenerational Oral History Projects.* Walnut Creek, CA: Left Coast Press.

Transcribing and Editing Guides

Minnesota Historical Society. Oral History Office. 2001. Transcribing, Editing and Processing Guidelines. St. Paul: Minnesota Historical Society. www.mnhs.org/collections/oralhistory/ohtranscribing.pdf.

Baylor University Institute for Oral History. 2013. Style Guide: A Quick Guide for Editing Oral History Transcripts. www.baylor.edu/oralhistory/doc.php/14142.pdf.

Images and Using Objects Guides

Australian Centre for the Moving Image: www.acmi.net.au/.

Center for Digital Storytellng: http://storycenter.org/.

Freund, Alexander and Alistair Thomson eds. 2011. *Oral History and Photography.* New York: Palgrave.

Stein, Jesse Adams. 2013. "'That Was a Posed Photo': Reflections on the Process of Combining Oral Histories with Institutional Photographs." *Oral History Association of Australia Journal* 35: 49–57.

Wilton, Janis. 2008. "Telling Objects: Material Culture and Memory in Oral History Interviews." *Oral History Association of Australia Journal* 30: 41–49.

Legal and Ethical Issues

Australian Copyright Council: www.copyright.org.au/.

Code of Best Practices in Fair Use for Academic and Research Libraries. Association of Research Libraries, 2012. www.arl.org/storage/documents/publications/code-of-best-practices-fair-use.pdf.

Copyright and Fair Use. Stanford, CA: Center for the Internet and Society, Stanford Law School. http://cyberlaw.stanford.edu/focus-areas/copyright-and-fair-use.

Creative Commons. Includes instructions for creative commons options, a decision tree for choosing a license, the icons to add to your work, and blogs and discussions. http://us.creativecommons.org/.

Crews, Kenneth D. Permissions. New York, NY: Copyright Advisory Office, Columbia University. http://copyright.columbia.edu/copyright/permissions/.

Dougherty, Jack and Candace Simpson. 2012. "Who Owns Oral History? A Creative Commons Solution." In *Oral History in the Digital Age*, edited by Doug Boyd, Steve Cohen, Brad Rakerd, and Dean Rehberger. Washington, DC: Institute of Museum and Library Services. http://ohda.matrix.msu.edu/2012/06/a-creative-commons-solution/.

Larson, Mary A. 2013. "Steering Clear of the Rocks: A Look at the Current State of Oral History Ethics in the Digital Age." *Oral History Review* 40 (1): 36–49. DOI: 10.1093/ohr/oht028.

Neuenschwander, John A. 2014. *A Guide to Oral History and the Law.* 2nd ed. Oxford: Oxford University Press.

Stim, Richard. 2013. *Getting Permission: How to License & Clear Copyrighted Materials Online & Off.* 5th ed. Berkeley, CA: Nolo Press.

United States Copyright Office. Copyright Basics. www.copyright.gov/circs/circ01.pdf. Twelve page brochure answering all the basic questions about copyright.

Recording Technology

ARSC Recorded Sound Discussion List. Unmoderated discussion for sound recording preservation at all levels. www.arsc-audio.org/arsclist.html.

Bennett, Hugh. 2013. *Understanding CD-R and CD-RW: Physical, Logical and File System Standards.* Cupertino, CA: Optical Storage Technology Association. www.osta.org/technology/pdf/cdr_cdrw.pdf.

Boyd, Douglas A. 2012. "Audio or Video for Recording Oral History: Questions, Decisions." In *Oral History in the Digital Age*, edited by Doug Boyd, Steve Cohen, Brad Rakerd, and Dean Rehberger. Washington, DC: Institute of Museum and Library Services. http://ohda.matrix.msu.edu/2012/06/audio-or-video-for-recording-oral-history/.

Hay, Joanna. 2012. "Case Study: Using Video in Oral History—Learning from One Woman's Experiences." In *Oral History in the Digital Age*, edited by Doug Boyd, Steve Cohen, Brad Rakerd, and Dean Rehberger. Washington, DC: Institute of Museum and Library Services. http://ohda.matrix.msu.edu/2012/06/using-video-in-oral-history/.

Historical Voices. 2002. *Oral History Tutorial: Audio Technology.* East Lansing, MI: MATRIX, Michigan State University. www.historicalvoices.org/oralhistory/audio-tech.html.

Morton, David L. 2006. *Sound Recording: The Life Story of a Technology.* Baltimore, MD: Johns Hopkins University.

Professional Standards and Best Practices

An Internet search on the organization and title will retrieve best practices for each organization.

American Association of State and Local History. Statement of Professional Standards and Ethics. Updated 2012.

American Historical Association. Statement on standards of professional conduct. Updated 2011.

National Council on Public History. Bylaws and Ethics. Adopted 2007.

Oral History Association. Principles and Best Practices. Adopted October 2009.

Society of American Archivists. SAA Core Values Statement and Code of Ethics. Rev. 2011.

Digital Preservation

Byers, Fred R. 2003. *Care and Handling of CDs and DVDs: A Guide for Librarians and Archivists*. Washington, DC: CLIR. www.itl.nist.gov/iad/894.05/docs/ CDandDVDCareandHandlingGuide.pdf.

Casey, Mike, and Bruce Gordon. 2007. *Sound Directions: Best Practices for Audio Preservation*. Bloomington: Indiana University; Boston: Harvard University. www. dlib.indiana.edu/projects/sounddirections/papersPresent/sd_bp_07.pdf.

Digital Curation Centre. www.dcc.ac.uk/. A UK-based center of expertise on all aspects of digital curation. Many resources on the website, including how-to guides, publications, and an international conference.

Guidelines on the Production and Preservation of Digital Audio Objects: Report# IASA-TC04, 2nd ed. IASA, 2009.

LOCKSS (Lots of Copies Keeps Stuff Safe). Open source software for libraries and archives for preserving and providing access to digital collections. www.lockss. org/.

National Recording Preservation Board of the Library of Congress. Audio Preservation Bibliography. 2014. www.loc.gov/rr/record/nrpb/nrpb-presbib.html.

Oral Histories on the Internet

Cohen, Daniel J. and Roy Rosenzweig. 2006. *Digital History: A Guide to Gathering, Preserving and Presenting the Past on the Web*. Philadelphia: University of Pennsylvania Press. www.chnm.gmu.edu/digitalhistory. http://chnm.gmu.edu/digitalhistory/. Also available in print.

INDEX

Page numbers in *italics* refer to illustrations.

About the Author

Carol McKirdy is proprietor of the oral history consulting company History Herstory based in Sydney, Australia. She has conducted numerous oral history projects through adult education, communities, and societies, including an extensive project with a Sudanese immigrant community in Australia. She has been involved in oral history curriculum development for vocational training, runs an educational oral history wiki website, and is active in the Australian oral history community. Carol has a Master of Studies in Education from the University of Wollongong and has decades of experience teaching history and languages and literacy in secondary schools and adult education. Stories told by her adult education students inspired her to work in oral history. She adapted many student oral histories into lesson materials for other students studying social inclusion and vocational access courses. Other oral history projects include interviews with elderly Australian professional golfers, Chinese life stories, interviews with former members of the Australian Army, and distinguished educators.